PLAYS FOR PERFORMANCE

*A series designed for
contemporary production and study
Edited by
Nicholas Rudall and Bernard Sahlins*

HENRIK IBSEN

An Enemy of
the People

*In a New Translation and Adaptation by
Nicholas Rudall*

Ivan R. Dee
CHICAGO

Library of Congress Cataloging-in-Publication Data:
Ibsen, Henrik, 1828–1906.
    [Folkefiende English.]
    An enemy of the people / Henrik Ibsen ; In a New Translation and Adaptation by Nicholas Rudall.
        p. cm. — (Plays for performance)
    Includes bibliographical references and index.
    ISBN-13: 978-1-56663-727-5 (pbk. : alk. paper)
    ISBN-10: 1-56663-727-9 (pbk. : alk. paper)
    I. Rudall, Nicholas. II. Title. PT8862.A375 2007
    839.8'226—dc22
                                        2007005256

INTRODUCTION

by Nicholas Rudall

Ibsen wrote *An Enemy of the People*, significantly, in self-imposed exile in Rome in 1882. I say "significantly" because the hostile reception *Ghosts* had received in Scandinavia had soured him against the "liberal" press, and Ibsen subsequently left his homeland. This biographical fact is important to an understanding of this extraordinarily prescient play. The first two acts suggest an alliance between a charismatic physician, Dr. Stockmann, who has initially promoted a local spa and then discovered its potential toxicity, and the liberal elements in the town. It seems at first that the alliance between the doctor and the liberal press is on solid ground. But Ibsen gives the play its greatness by reversing all expectations. Those who supported the doctor turn on him, and his wife, who had been fearful of her family's future, embraces his courage.

Dr. Stockmann challenges the community not merely by attacking its venal and pusillanimous politicians but also by arguing that the real toxicity in the town is not in the sewage system but in the ignorance of the "solid majority," the mob. By assuming this seemingly elitist position, the doctor is branded an enemy of the people, his house is stoned, and he is left penniless.

3

This translation is designed for the spoken word. Each character has his or her quirks of diction, and although the subject matter is deeply felt and deeply serious, Ibsen introduces humor—even a touch of farce—into his rich text.

CHARACTERS

DR. THOMAS STOCKMANN, medical officer at the
Municipal Baths

MRS. KATHERINE STOCKMANN

PETRA, their daughter, a schoolteacher

EILIF, their son, age thirteen

MORTEN, their son, age ten

PETER STOCKMANN, Thomas's elder brother, the
mayor and chief constable of this small town,
and chairman of the Municipal Baths
Committee

MORTEN KIIL, a tanner in the local hide industry and
stepfather of Mrs. Stockmann

HOVSTAD, editor of the local paper, *The People's
Tribune*

BILLING, an employee of that newspaper

HORSTER, a sea captain

ASLAKSEN, a printer

PEOPLE AT THE PUBLIC MEETING. Ibsen specifies that
they should be of all classes and all ages; there
should be some women and a number of
schoolboys.

A town by the sea in southern Norway.

An Enemy of the People

ACT 1

It is evening. Dr. Stockmann's living room, neatly furnished but not lavish. There are two doors to the right. The farther one leads into the hallway. The nearer leads into the doctor's study. On the other wall is another door which leads into the family quarters.

A tiled stove stands in the middle of this part of the house. A sofa has a mirror above it. In front of the sofa is an oval table covered by a cloth. On it is a lamp, lighted and with a shade.

To the back (upstage) is an open door revealing the dining room. The dining table is laid for the evening meal. A lamp is on the table.

Billing is seated at the table, a napkin tucked under his chin. Mrs. Stockmann is offering a plate of roast beef. The other places are empty. It looks like the end of a meal.

MRS. STOCKMANN: There you are, Mr. Billing. But if you're an hour late you'll have to put up with cold meat.

BILLING: (*eating*) This is wonderful. . . . Wonderful!

MRS. STOCKMANN: Thomas always likes to eat on time . . . as you know.

BILLING: It doesn't bother me. I actually enjoy eating by myself. Don't have to talk to anyone.

9

MRS. STOCKMANN: Ah well, as long as you're enjoying it, that's the main . . . (*hears a noise in the hall*) Ah, that must be Mr. Hovstad.

BILLING: Probably.

(*Mayor Peter Stockmann enters. He is wearing an overcoat and his mayor's hat. He also has a walking stick.*)

MAYOR: (*from the living room*) Good evening, Katherine!

MRS. STOCKMANN: (*entering*) Oh, it's you. How nice of you to come and see us.

MAYOR: I was just passing, so . . . (*looking upstage*) but you have company. . . .

MRS. STOCKMANN: No. No no no. . . . He just stopped by. . . . Won't you have a little bite?

MAYOR: Me? No, thank you. No cooked meals at night for me. Digestion problems.

MRS. STOCKMANN: Oh, but just for once. . . .

MAYOR: No, no. . . . That's very kind of you. I stick to bread and butter at this time of night. It's healthier . . . and cheaper.

MRS. STOCKMANN: Are you suggesting that Thomas and I spend too much money?

MAYOR: Not you, my dear. It never entered my mind. (*looking at the study*) Isn't he in?

MRS. STOCKMANN: No, he's gone for a walk with the boys.

MAYOR: So soon after dinner? Not wise. . . . (*hears a noise*) Ah, that must be him.

MRS. STOCKMANN: No. I think not yet. (*a knock at the door*) Come in!

(*Hovstad enters*)

MRS. STOCKMANN: Oh, Mr. Hovstad!

HOVSTAD: Yes. Excuse me. Little bit late. I was at the printer's. Good evening, Mr. Mayor.

MAYOR: Good evening. (*formally*) You have some business here?

HOVSTAD: Yes, some. It's about an article in my newspaper.

MAYOR: I thought it might be. My brother seems to be a regular contributor to the *People's Tribune*. . . .

HOVSTAD: Yes. He writes for us quite often. Especially when there is a need to tell the truth about something.

MRS. STOCKMANN: (*pointing to the dining room*) Would you like something to . . .

MAYOR: I understand. Of course. I don't blame him for writing articles that will win him immediate sympathy from his readers. And of course I bear no antipathy to your paper, Mr. Hovstad.

HOVSTAD: I hope not, sir.

MAYOR: On the whole I think it is fair to say that we are a tolerant and open community. We *are* a community. We have a common interest that makes us one. And it is a great interest which every right-minded citizen takes to his . . .

HOVSTAD: You mean the baths?

MAYOR: Exactly. Our magnificent new Municipal Baths. Now listen to me, sir. These baths will be our heart. They will be the soul of our town and our life here. There is no doubt.

11

MRS. STOCKMANN: That's what Thomas says. . . .

MAYOR: It's remarkable what this town has achieved in the past two or three years. We have become prosperous. People seem alive again. They thrive. Property values go up every day.

HOVSTAD: And there are fewer people unemployed.

MAYOR: That is true, too. Those who own property have a reduced obligation to help the poor. . . . That is welcome news, especially if we have a really good summer this year. Lots of visitors. Invalids are what we need. They'll put the baths on the map.

HOVSTAD: I hear that the prospects are good.

MAYOR: They are. People are inquiring about accommodations every day.

HOVSTAD: Well then, the doctor's article will be . . . timely.

MAYOR: Something new?

HOVSTAD: No, something he wrote last winter. It was a panegyric of the baths. He praised the health facilities, but I decided not to publish it.

MAYOR: A problem?

HOVSTAD: No, I decided to wait until spring. Now people are thinking about their summer vacations.

MAYOR: Mr. Hovstad, you are so right, so right.

MRS. STOCKMANN: Thomas never stops thinking about those Municipal Baths.

MAYOR: Well, that's where he works.

HOVSTAD: And he made it, didn't he? He created it?

MAYOR: Did he? Really? Some people seem to think so. I have to say that I was partially under the impression that I had some minor share in its formation.

MRS. STOCKMANN: Thomas always says that you did.

HOVSTAD: Mr. Mayor, we all agree that your influence was huge. You initiated it . . . you got all the practical details in place. We all know that. What I mean is that Dr. Stockmann got the idea first.

MAYOR: Yes. He has always been full of ideas, my brother. Unfortunately. But when you have to *do* things, Mr. Hovstad, you need a man of action . . . and in this house that is not particularly . . .

MRS. STOCKMANN: Mr. Mayor, Peter, would you like to . . . ?

HOVSTAD: Surely you don't think that . . . ?

MRS. STOCKMANN: Please go in and get yourself something to eat, Mr. Hovstad. My husband will be home anytime soon.

HOVSTAD: Well, thank you, just a nibble perhaps. (*goes into the dining room*)

MAYOR: (*lowering his voice*) The working class! No tact. They don't know the meaning of the word.

MRS. STOCKMANN: But is this anything to worry about? You and Thomas are brothers. You can share the honor.

MAYOR: I would have thought so. However, not everyone seems to be willing to share.

MRS. STOCKMANN: Oh nonsense! You and Thomas get on so well together. Ah, that sounds like him. (*opens door that leads to the entrance hall*)

DR. STOCKMANN: (*laughing and full of himself*) Katherine, my dear! We've got another guest! The more the merrier, I say. Come in, Captain Horster. Put your overcoat on the hook. Stupid of me. You don't wear an overcoat! I bumped into him on the street! You have no idea how difficult it was to persuade him to come back here with me!

(*Captain Horster enters and shakes hands with Mrs. Stockmann. Eilif and Morten trail behind. Dr. Stockmann is still in the doorway.*)

DR. STOCKMANN: Go go. . . . Go on in, my boys! (*to Mrs. Stockmann*) They're hungry already. Go in there, Captain Horster . . . you're going to have the best roast beef you ever . . . (*herds all three of them into the dining room*)

MRS. STOCKMANN: Thomas! Don't you see who's . . . ?

DR. STOCKMANN: Oh Peter! (*shakes his hand*) So good to see you!

MAYOR: I'm afraid I have to leave in a few minutes. . . .

DR. STOCKMANN: Nonsense! A quick glass of hot toddy first. You didn't forget it, Katherine, did you?

MRS. STOCKMANN: Of course not. The kettle is boiling. (*goes to the dining room*)

MAYOR: Hot toddy! Well . . .

DR. STOCKMANN: Yes. Now sit down and we'll have a good time.

MAYOR: Thank you. But parties with alcoholic beverages are something I do not indulge in.

DR. STOCKMANN: This isn't a party.

MAYOR: Well, but . . . (*looks toward the dining room*) It amazes me how much they can eat.

DR. STOCKMANN: (*rubbing his hands*) Yes, there's nothing better than to see young people down their food. . . . That's how it should be! They need food . . . gives 'em strength. They're the ones who have to find the primal energy for our future.

MAYOR: May I ask what this "primal energy," as you put it, will be applied to?

DR. STOCKMANN: Well, you have to ask *them* that . . . when the time comes. We can't see that of course . . . a couple of old has-beens like us.

MAYOR: That seems to me an extraordinary way to categorize us.

DR. STOCKMANN: I was joking, Peter. You see . . . I feel so happy, exhilarated even. This is a wonderful time to be alive. There is energy and it *is* primal. The world is . . . seeding itself. It *is* a great time to be alive. It's a birth—no, a rebirth. And it's happening before our eyes.

MAYOR: Do you really feel that?

DR. STOCKMANN: Yes, I do. You can't see it as I do. Not as clearly. You've spent your life here, in this small town. So you have a different perspective on change from me. . . . I've had to spend the best years of my life in that . . . isolation up north. I never saw a new face. Ever. No one who could challenge my mind. To come here for me is to come into the heart of a huge city.

MAYOR: A city . . . ?

DR. STOCKMANN: Oh I know it must *seem* small . . . I mean in comparison with other cities. But for me . . . there's life here . . . a future . . . things to work for . . . things to fight for. (*shouts*) Has the mail come?

MRS. STOCKMANN: No, not yet.

DR. STOCKMANN: And I make a decent living, Peter. That means something when we have been living on the edge of poverty . . . as we have.

MAYOR: Please . . . !

DR. STOCKMANN: Oh yes we have. Sometimes we didn't know where the next piece of change would come from.

MAYOR: Surely that's not . . .

DR. STOCKMANN: Oh yes. We were at times on the edge. But now we can live like the rich. Today, for example, we had a whole beef roast. And there were leftovers. We could feed our friends. Have some. At least let me bring you in. Come and see. . . .

MAYOR: No. Really.

DR. STOCKMANN: We have a tablecloth.

MAYOR: So I see.

DR. STOCKMANN: And a lamp with a shade. It's Katherine. She manages to save quite a bit and can buy things like these. The room seems so cozy, don't you think? Come and stand over here—no no no, not there! Now look. See how the light focuses downward? I think it really looks elegant, don't you?

MAYOR: Well, if you can indulge in that sort of luxury. . . .

DR. STOCKMANN: I think I can allow myself a little at the present. Katherine says that I earn almost as much as we spend.

MAYOR: Almost?!

DR. STOCKMANN: Well, a man of science ought to live in a little luxury. I'm sure that a magistrate spends far more in a year than I do.

MAYOR: Yes, I would hope so. After all, a magistrate is an important public official. . . .

DR. STOCKMANN: Well, let's say a merchant then. . . . A businessman spends much more than . . .

MAYOR: Well, he can afford to. . . .

DR. STOCKMANN: It's not that I'm wasteful, Peter. I just need the pleasure of having people around me. I need it. I have lived apart from this world for so long, and for me, well, I need to be with young people, who have courage, and can laugh, and have open, inquisitive minds. And that is precisely what they have . . . all those men in there enjoying a good meal. I wish you knew Hovstad a little better. . . .

MAYOR: Which reminds me . . . Hovstad told me he's going to print another article by you.

DR. STOCKMANN: An article?

MAYOR: Yes, about the baths. Something you wrote last winter.

DR. STOCKMANN: Oh, that! No. I don't want them to print that at the moment.

MAYOR: No? But I would have thought that this would be the perfect time.

DR. STOCKMANN: Well, yes . . . if the circumstances were different. (*crosses the room*)

MAYOR: (*watching him*) How do you mean different?

DR. STOCKMANN: (*stops*) Sorry, Peter, I can't talk about it yet. Not tonight, anyway. There may be a great deal that's . . . out of the ordinary. Or maybe it's nothing at all. It may be all in my imagination.

17

MAYOR: You're making it all sound very mysterious, I must say. What's the matter? You can't tell me? I would have thought that, as chairman of the Municipal Baths Committee, I . . .

DR. STOCKMANN: And I would have thought that I . . . as the . . . Well, let's not get worked up about it.

MAYOR: God forbid! I'm not in the habit of getting worked up about things, as you put it. But I must insist that all negotiations be made in consultation with the proper authorities, those legally appointed to do so. I cannot allow anything underhanded or surreptitious.

DR. STOCKMANN: Have I ever been underhanded or surreptitious?

MAYOR: You've always done things your way. And that is not very appropriate in a structured society. The individual must learn to fall in line with public opinion . . . or to be more accurate, with the opinion of the authorities appointed to watch over the common good.

DR. STOCKMANN: I'm sure. But what the hell has that got to do with me?

MAYOR: My dear Thomas . . . that is precisely what you never seem willing to learn. But be careful. It will come back to haunt you one day. Well, I've warned you. Good night.

DR. STOCKMANN: Are you out of your mind? You're fishing in the wrong stream.

MAYOR: I'm not in the habit of doing that. Well, if you'll excuse me. . . . (*with a bow at the dining room door*) Goodbye, Katherine. Good evening, gentlemen. (*leaves*)

MRS. STOCKMANN: (*entering the living room*) Has he gone?

DR. STOCKMANN: Yes, dear, he has, and in a damned foul mood.

MRS. STOCKMANN: Thomas, what did you do this time?

DR. STOCKMANN: Nothing at all. He can't expect me to be accountable to him . . . until the time comes.

MRS. STOCKMANN: Accountable to him? What for?

(*Hovstad, Billing, and Horster leave the dining room and enter. Eilif and Morten follow shortly after.*)

BILLING: (*stretching his arms*) Aah. A meal like that makes you feel like a new man. By golly, yesiree.

HOVSTAD: His Honor the Mayor wasn't in a very good mood tonight.

DR. STOCKMANN: That's his stomach. He has indigestion.

HOVSTAD: Perhaps we stuck in his throat, radical journalists that we are.

MRS. STOCKMANN: I thought you were getting on rather well with him.

HOVSTAD: It's just a truce.

BILLING: That's it! The word sums up the situation completely.

DR. STOCKMANN: Peter is a very lonely man. I feel sorry for him. We must remember that. He has no home to go to where he can just relax. It's business, business all the time. And all that damn tea he pours down his throat. Well, my men, pull up your chairs. Katherine, where's the hot toddy?

MRS. STOCKMANN: (*going into the dining room*) Just coming!

DR. STOCKMANN: Sit here on the sofa with me, Captain Horster. You're too rare a visitor in this house. Sit, sit, gentlemen.

(*They sit at the table. Mrs. Stockmann brings a tray with a kettle, decanters, glasses, etc.*)

MRS. STOCKMANN: Here we are. This is arrak . . . this is rum, and that's the brandy. Everyone help themselves.

DR. STOCKMANN: (*taking a glass*) Don't worry about that! (*as the toddy is being mixed*) Where are the cigars? Eilif, you know where the box is. Morten, you can get me my pipe. (*the boys go into the room on the right*) I have a suspicion that Eilif sneaks a cigar now and again . . . but I pretend I don't know. (*shouting*) Morten! Bring my smoking cap, too! Katherine, can you tell him where I put it? Oh good, he's found it. (*the boys come back with everything*) Help yourselves, my friends. I'll stick to my pipe. This old thing has been my friend on many a stormy night on my rounds up there in the north. (*clinks glasses*) Cheers! Aah! It's so much nicer to be sitting here relaxed and warm.

MRS. STOCKMANN: (*sitting and knitting*) Will you be sailing soon, Captain Horster?

HORSTER: I expect to be leaving next week.

MRS. STOCKMANN: America this time, isn't it?

HORSTER: That's it.

BILLING: But you won't be able to vote in the next council elections.

HORSTER: There's going to be new elections?

BILLING: You didn't know?

HORSTER: No, I'm not really interested. . . .

BILLING: But you must care about the city's business?

HORSTER: No, I don't really understand what's going on.

BILLING: All the same, at least you ought to vote.

HORSTER: Even if you don't understand what's going on?

BILLING: Understand? What's that got to do with it? Our society is like a ship. Everyone should have a hand on the helm.

HORSTER: Not on my ship!

HOVSTAD: Strange how little sailors care about what's going on in their own country.

BILLING: Quite bizarre.

DR. STOCKMANN: Sailors are like migrating birds: wherever they happen to be, they treat that as their home. Which means that the rest of us must take an even greater interest in things, Mr. Hovstad. Are you publishing anything stimulating in tomorrow's *People's Tribune?*

HOVSTAD: Nothing of any local interest. But I thought of printing your article in a couple of days. . . .

DR. STOCKMANN: Oh God, yes, that article! No, look, you'll have to just sit on that.

HOVSTAD: Really? We've got plenty of space at the moment. And I thought this would be a good time. . . .

DR. STOCKMANN: Yes, yes, you're probably right, but you'll just have to wait. . . . I'll explain later.

(Petra, in her hat and cloak, with a pile of exercise books, enters from the hall)

PETRA: Good evening!

DR. STOCKMANN: Petra, that you?

(The others greet her. She puts her books, cloak, and hat on a chair.)

PETRA: You're all sitting around having a party while I've been out slaving away!

DR. STOCKMANN: Then join the party.

BILLING: May I fix you a small glass?

PETRA: No thanks, I'll do it myself. You always make it too strong. Oh, by the way, Father, I've got a letter for you. . . .

(goes to chair)

DR. STOCKMANN: A letter? Who from?

PETRA: *(looking in her coat pocket)* The mailman gave it to me as I was going out.

DR. STOCKMANN: Why the devil didn't you give it to me before?

PETRA: I really didn't have time to run upstairs again. Here we are.

DR. STOCKMANN: *(taking it)* Let me see it, child, let me see it. *(looking at envelope)* Yes, this is it!

MRS. STOCKMANN: Is this the one you've been so anxious about, Thomas?

DR. STOCKMANN: Yes, it is. I must go to my room and read it at once. A lamp! Katherine, is there a lamp in my room?

MRS. STOCKMANN: Yes, there's one lit on your desk.

DR. STOCKMANN: Good, good. Excuse me for a moment. (*goes into his study*)

PETRA: What do you think that is, Mother?

MRS. STOCKMANN: I've no idea. For the last couple of days he hasn't stopped asking about the mailman.

BILLING: Probably some patient from out of town.

PETRA: Poor old Dad. One of these days he'll work himself to death. (*mixes a glass*) Ah! That tastes good!

HOVSTAD: Have you been teaching night school?

PETRA: (*sipping her drink*) Two hours.

BILLING: And four hours at school this morning?

PETRA: (*sitting at the table*) Five.

MRS. STOCKMANN: And you've got exercises to correct tonight, too?

PETRA: Yes, a pile.

HORSTER: You seem to be working too hard yourself.

PETRA: Yes, but I like it. It makes me so blissfully tired.

BILLING: And you like that?

PETRA: Yes, you sleep so soundly after that.

MORTEN: You must be really wicked, Petra.

PETRA: Wicked?

MORTEN: Yes, if you work so much. Dr. Roerlund says that work is a punishment for our sins.

EILIF: Stupid! To believe stuff like that!

MRS. STOCKMANN: Now, now, Eilif.

BILLING: (*laughing*) Very good. Very good!

HOVSTAD: Don't you want to work as hard as your sister, Morten?

MORTEN: No, sir! Not me!

HOVSTAD: What do you want to be then?

MORTEN: A Viking would be great.

EILIF: Then you'd be a heathen!

MORTEN: All right, I'll be a heathen.

BILLING: I'm with you, Morten. My sentiments exactly.

MRS. STOCKMANN: (*gesturing to him*) I'm sure you don't mean that, Mr. Billing.

BILLING: I swear to you I do. I *am* a heathen, and proud of it. It won't be long before we all become heathens. You'll see.

MORTEN: Will we be able to do anything we want then?

BILLING: Yes, Morten. You see . . .

MRS. STOCKMANN: Hurry along now, boys. I'm sure you've got some homework to do.

EILIF: Can I stay a little bit longer?

MRS. STOCKMANN: No, you can't. Off you go, the pair of you!

(*they say good night and leave*)

HOVSTAD: Do you think it's bad for the boys to hear this kind of thing?

MRS. STOCKMANN: Oh, I don't know. I just don't like it.

PETRA: Oh, Mother! I think that's a little silly.

MRS. STOCKMANN: Maybe it is. I just don't like it. Not here, in the house.

PETRA: Everyone is afraid of the truth. At home, at school. . . . At home we have to keep our mouths shut, and at school we must stand up and tell lies to the children.

HORSTER: Lies?

PETRA: Yes. Don't you realize that we have to teach them all kinds of things that we don't believe ourselves?

BILLING: I'm afraid that's all too true.

PETRA: If I had the money, I'd start a school of my own. . . . There things would be different.

BILLING: Ah yes, money!

HORSTER: Well, Miss Stockmann, if you really mean that, I would gladly give you a classroom of your own. My father's old house is almost empty, and there's this huge dining room downstairs—

PETRA: (*laughing*) Thank you, but I'm afraid nothing will come of it.

HOVSTAD: No, I think Miss Petra will become a journalist. By the way, have you had time to take a look at that English novel you promised to translate for us?

PETRA: Not yet. But you'll have it on time.

(*Dr. Stockmann enters with the letter in his hand*)

DR. STOCKMANN: (*waving the letter*) Here's something that will give this town something to talk about, I can tell you.

BILLING: Some news?

MRS. STOCKMANN: What's happened?

DR. STOCKMANN: A great discovery, Katherine!

HOVSTAD: Really?

MRS. STOCKMANN: You made it?

DR. STOCKMANN: I did indeed. (*walks up and down*) Now let them come and say that it's all the ravings of a lunatic and I'm imagining things as usual. But they'll have to be careful this time, I can tell you.

PETRA: Father, tell us what it is!

DR. STOCKMANN: Yes, yes. Just give me a moment and then I'll tell you. Oh, if only Peter were here now! Well, it only goes to show how blind we human beings are. We make judgments in the dark.

HOVSTAD: What do you mean by that, Doctor?

DR. STOCKMANN: (*standing by the table*) The general and popular view is that our town is a healthy place, isn't it?

HOVSTAD: Of course.

DR. STOCKMANN: A remarkably healthy place? A place which deserves its glowing reputation as a spa for the sick and indeed for the healthy?

MRS. STOCKMANN: Yes, but my dear Thomas—

DR. STOCKMANN: I myself have praised it, recommended it, haven't I? I have written thousands of words about it. Accolades! In the *Tribune*, in pamphlets. . . .

HOVSTAD: So?

DR. STOCKMANN: These baths, which have been called "the main artery" of the town, "its central nervous system," and—and God knows what else—

BILLING: "The throbbing heart of the city" was something I came up with on some festive occasion or other—

26

DR. STOCKMANN: I'm sure you did. But do you know what they really are, these beloved, much-praised baths of ours, which cost so much money? Do you know what they are?

HOVSTAD: No. What?

MRS. STOCKMANN: Yes, what are they?

DR. STOCKMANN: A filthy cesspool!

(*all together*)

PETRA: The baths, Father?

MRS. STOCKMANN: Our baths!

HOVSTAD: But Doctor—

BILLING: Absolutely incredible!

DR. STOCKMANN: The baths are a marble tomb—and a poisonous one, too! Presenting the gravest possible danger to the public. All that filth up at Moelledal—I must tell you . . . that stinking drainage from the tanneries has infected the water in the pipes, which supply the pump room. And the same damned poison has even drained onto the beach.

HORSTER: Into the sea baths?

DR. STOCKMANN: Exactly.

HOVSTAD: How can you be sure about this, Doctor?

DR. STOCKMANN: I have made a thorough investigation of the whole thing. Oh, I've been suspicious for a long time. Last year there were a lot of strange complaints from visitors to the spa—typhoid and gastric fever—

MRS. STOCKMANN: Yes, there were.

DR. STOCKMANN: At the time we thought these people were already infected when they came here. Later on, during the winter, I began to have second thoughts. So I determined to analyze the water as best I could.

MRS. STOCKMANN: So, that's why you've been so busy.

DR. STOCKMANN: Indeed, I have been busy, Katherine. But of course I didn't have the proper scientific equipment. So I sent samples of the drinking water and seawater to the university to have them analyzed by a chemist.

HOVSTAD: And now you have the results?

DR. STOCKMANN: (*showing the letter*) Here they are! This proves beyond a reasonable doubt that the water contains decomposing organic matter—millions of bacteria. Without a doubt the water is toxic whether you drink it or wash with it.

MRS. STOCKMANN: Thank God you found this out in time.

DR. STOCKMANN: You may well say so, Katherine.

HOVSTAD: And what do you intend to do now, Doctor?

DR. STOCKMANN: Put things right, of course.

HOVSTAD: Can that be done?

DR. STOCKMANN: It *has* to be done! Otherwise the baths will be totally unusable and all our work will be wasted. But not to worry, I have a pretty good idea of what needs to be done.

MRS. STOCKMANN: But, my dear, why have you kept it all so secret?

DR. STOCKMANN: Do you think I'd go around town talking about this before I had absolute proof? No, thank you. I'm not that much of a fool.

PETRA: But you might have told us—

DR. STOCKMANN: I wasn't telling anyone. But in the morning you can run round to the old Badger's place . . .

MRS. STOCKMANN: Thomas! Really!

DR. STOCKMANN: Sorry! I mean to your grandfather's—he'll be shocked out of his wits. He thinks I'm a bit soft in the head anyway—oh and lots of people think so, too! I know! But now all these fine folk are going to see. They'll see. (*walking about and rubbing his hands*) There's going to be such an uproar in this town. Katherine! You've no idea! All the water conduits will have to be relaid.

HOVSTAD: (*getting up*) All of them?

DR. STOCKMANN: Of course. The intake points are too low. They'll have to be raised to a much higher level.

PETRA: Then you were right after all.

DR. STOCKMANN: Yes, Petra, you remember! I wrote to protest the plans when they were about to start laying the pipes. But no one would listen. Well, this time I'll attack on all fronts. I've already written a full report to the Baths Committee. It's been ready to go for a week. I've just been waiting for this. (*shows letter*) But now I'll send it to them right away. (*goes to his room, returns with a sheaf of papers*) Look at this. Ten full-sized pages . . . small handwriting. And I'm sending the test results with it. Katherine, get me a sheet of newspaper. Something to wrap these in. . . . Good! There, now, give it to . . . to . . . damn it, what's her name? You know, the maid. Tell her to take it straight down to the mayor. (*Mrs. Stockmann goes into the dining room with the package*)

PETRA: What do you think Uncle Peter will say, Father?

DR. STOCKMANN: Well, what can he say? He has to be thankful that an issue of this importance has seen the light of day.

HOVSTAD: May I have your permission to print a short piece on your findings in the *Tribune?*

DR. STOCKMANN: I'd be grateful if you would.

HOVSTAD: I think the community needs this information as soon as possible.

DR. STOCKMANN: Yes, of course.

MRS. STOCKMANN: (*enters*) She's taken it with her.

BILLING: You'll be the town's leading citizen. By golly, Doctor, yesiree.

DR. STOCKMANN: (*walking around smiling*) Oh, nonsense. All I've done is my duty. I went digging and got lucky, that's all. All the same . . .

BILLING: Hovstad, don't you think the town ought to organize a torchlight parade or something to honor Dr. Stockmann?

HOVSTAD: Well, I'll certainly make that proposal.

BILLING: And I'll talk to Aslaksen.

DR. STOCKMANN: No, no, my dear friends. Don't bother with all that nonsense. No fuss! And if the Baths Committee offers to raise my salary, I won't accept. No. It's no good, Katherine, I just won't accept it.

MRS. STOCKMANN: Quite right, Thomas.

PETRA: (*raising her glass*) Your health, Father.

HOVSTAD AND BILLING: Your health, Doctor.

HORSTER: (*clinking glasses with the doctor*) Here's hoping that what you have done will bring you nothing but happiness.

DR. STOCKMANN: Thank you, my dear friends, thank you. I am truly happy. It is a good feeling to know you have the respect of your fellow citizens. Hey, ho, Katherine.

(*Dr. Stockmann puts his arms around Mrs. Stockmann's neck and spins her around. She screams with laughter and tries to escape. Laughter, cheers, applause. The boys stick their heads around the door.*)

ACT 2

It is morning. The living room. The dining room door is closed.

MRS. STOCKMANN: (*enters through the dining room with an envelope, goes to the door on the right, and peeps in*) Are you in, Thomas?

DR. STOCKMANN: Yes, I just got back. (*enters*) What is it?

MRS. STOCKMANN: A letter from your brother. (*gives it to him*)

DR. STOCKMANN: Aha! Let's see what he has to say. (*opens the letter and reads aloud*) I return herewith the manuscript you sent me . . . (*mumbling*) um, hum, hum . . .

MRS. STOCKMANN: Well, what does he have to say?

DR. STOCKMANN: (*putting the papers in his pocket*) He just says that he'll come and see me around noon.

MRS. STOCKMANN: Then you'd better not go out again.

DR. STOCKMANN: It's no problem. I finished my rounds for the day.

MRS. STOCKMANN: I'm really curious to see how he reacts.

DR. STOCKMANN: You'll see. He won't be too happy that I, not he, made this discovery.

MRS. STOCKMANN: And you're not worried? I am.

DR. STOCKMANN: Well, deep down, of course, he'll be happy. Only trouble is Peter gets so damned furious if anyone but he does anything good for the town.

MRS. STOCKMANN: You know, Thomas, why don't you share the credit with him? Couldn't you just say that . . . that it was he who started you thinking about this?

DR. STOCKMANN: I'd be glad to. All I want is to get everything put right.

MORTEN KIIL: (*sticks his head in from the hallway, looks in inquisitively, chuckles, and asks slyly*) Is it? Is it true?

DR. STOCKMANN: Hello, Morten, hello. Good morning. Good morning.

MRS. STOCKMANN: Aren't you going to come in?

MORTEN KIIL: I will if it's true. If it's not, I'm off.

DR. STOCKMANN: If what's true?

MORTEN KIIL: All this nonsense about the pipes. Is it true?

DR. STOCKMANN: Of course it's true. How did you hear about it?

MORTEN KIIL: (*coming into the room*) Petra stopped by on her way to school.

DR. STOCKMANN: Oh, did she?

MORTEN KIIL: Aha. And she told me. I thought she was joking. But she's not like that.

33

DR. STOCKMANN: Why do you think she would joke about a thing like that?

MORTEN KIIL: Never trust anyone, that's my motto. You're made a fool of before you know where you are. So, it's true?

DR. STOCKMANN: Absolutely true. Now sit down, Father. (*coaxes him to the sofa*) Isn't this lucky for the town?

MORTEN KIIL: (*stifling a laugh*) Lucky? For the town?!

DR. STOCKMANN: That I found all this out in time.

MORTEN KIIL: (*still chuckling*) Oh, yes, yes, yes. But I never thought you'd monkey around with your own family.

DR. STOCKMANN: Monkey around?

MRS. STOCKMANN: Father, dear!

MORTEN KIIL: (*rests his hands and chin on the handle of his walking stick and winks slyly at the Doctor*) Now, what was it? Didn't you say that some animals had gotten into the pipes?

DR. STOCKMANN: Yes, bacteria.

MORTEN KIIL: Quite a lot, Petra said. An army of them.

DR. STOCKMANN: Millions, probably.

MORTEN KIIL: But no one can see them, is that right?

DR. STOCKMANN: Of course you can't *see* them.

MORTEN KIIL: God damn it! This is the best yet. I mean, for you.

DR. STOCKMANN: What do you mean?

MORTEN KIIL: You'll never get the mayor to believe in all that.

DR. STOCKMANN: We'll see.

MORTEN KIIL: Do you think he's that stupid?

DR. STOCKMANN: I hope the whole town will be that stupid.

MORTEN KIIL: The whole town? Well, I wouldn't be surprised. They deserve it. Teach them a lesson. They hounded me out of the city council. That's right. Drove me out like a dog. But, now it's their turn. They're the idiots, Thomas.

DR. STOCKMANN: But Father . . .

MORTEN KIIL: Show them up for the idiots they are. (*gets up*) If you can take the mayor and his cronies down a peg or two, I'll give a hundred crowns to the Poor Fund right away.

DR. STOCKMANN: Very generous.

MORTEN KIIL: I'm not a rich man, mind you. But, if you pull this off, I'll remember the poor . . . maybe fifty at Christmas.

HOVSTAD: (*enters*) Good morning. Oh, am I intruding?

DR. STOCKMANN: No, come in, come in.

MORTEN KIIL: (*chuckling*) Aha! Is he in on this too?

HOVSTAD: What do you mean?

DR. STOCKMANN: Indeed he is.

MORTEN KIIL: I might have guessed. So, it's going to be in the papers. Yes, you're a clever one, all right, Stockmann. Well, you two put your heads together. I'm off.

DR. STOCKMANN: Oh, Father, stay a little longer.

MORTEN KIIL: No, I'm off. Don't spare them. Bamboozle them. By God, I'll make sure you won't regret it. (*goes, and Mrs. Stockmann goes with him*)

DR. STOCKMANN: (*laughing*) Can you believe it, Hovstad? The old man doesn't believe a word I say about the water system!

HOVSTAD: Oh, so *that* was what . . .

DR. STOCKMANN: Yes, that's what we were talking about. I guess that's why you've come too?

HOVSTAD: Yes. Can you spare me a moment or two, Doctor?

DR. STOCKMANN: All the time you want, my dear man.

HOVSTAD: Heard anything from the mayor?

DR. STOCKMANN: Not yet. He'll be coming by soon.

HOVSTAD: I've been thinking a lot about this. Since last night.

DR. STOCKMANN: Yes?

HOVSTAD: You're a doctor. A man of science. For you, this business about the pipes is something you think about as a separate entity. I mean, perhaps you don't realize how it's tied up with a lot of other things.

DR. STOCKMANN: I don't understand. Sit down, my dear man. No, over there on the sofa. (*Hovstad sits on the sofa, Dr. Stockmann in a chair opposite*) Well?

HOVSTAD: You said yesterday that the water pollution was the result of impurities in the soil.

DR. STOCKMANN: Yes, we can be pretty sure that the filth in the swamp at Moelledal is the reason for our problems.

36

HOVSTAD: Forgive me, Doctor, but I believe the real reason for our problems is to be found in a very different swamp.

DR. STOCKMANN: Which one?

HOVSTAD: The swamp in which our whole community is slowly decomposing.

DR. STOCKMANN: Damn it, Hovstad. What kind of talk is that?

HOVSTAD: Little by little all matters of importance in this town have fallen into the hands of a small pack of bureaucrats.

DR. STOCKMANN: Oh, come on. You can't put them all in that same box.

HOVSTAD: No, but the ones who are not in the box are the friends and cronies of the ones who are. It's the rich men, the ones people know. They're the ones who are running our lives.

DR. STOCKMANN: That's because they are clever, intelligent men.

HOVSTAD: Were they clever and intelligent when they laid down the water pipes?

DR. STOCKMANN: No. That was really stupid, of course. But now we can put it right.

HOVSTAD: Do you think they'll be happy about that?

DR. STOCKMANN: Happy or not, they'll have to do it.

HOVSTAD: If the press is allowed to influence the process.

DR. STOCKMANN: That won't be necessary, my dear man. I'm sure my brother will . . .

HOVSTAD: I'm sorry, Doctor. I intend to tackle this matter myself.

DR. STOCKMANN: In the newspaper?

HOVSTAD: When I accepted the editorship of the *Tribune,* I did so with the clear intention of breaking up this cabal of stubborn, narrow-minded power brokers in this town.

DR. STOCKMANN: But, as you told me, look what happened next! Your paper almost had to be shut down.

HOVSTAD: Well, yes. We had to play our cards right at that time. There was the risk that if these men were thrown out, the baths might not be built at all. But, now that we have the baths, these gentlemen have become . . . dispensable.

DR. STOCKMANN: Dispensable maybe, but we are in their debt nonetheless.

HOVSTAD: Oh, they'll have wonderful public recognition. But, I'm a radical, and a writer like me can't miss this opportunity. We must destroy the myth of these men's infallibility. It's a myth, and it must be exploded like any other.

DR. STOCKMANN: I'm with you there. If it's a myth, explode it.

HOVSTAD: I don't want to attack the mayor. He's your brother. But, I know that you feel as strongly as I do that the truth must be paramount.

DR. STOCKMANN: Of course. (*bursts out*) But . . . but . . . !

HOVSTAD: Don't think badly of me. I'm no more ambitious or self-obsessed than most people.

DR. STOCKMANN: My dear man, who says you are?

HOVSTAD: My parents were poor, as you know. I've been able to see what the lower classes of society need. They need to participate in public affairs—that's what will give them power, knowledge, and dignity.

DR. STOCKMANN: I agree.

HOVSTAD: I also think that a journalist has a lot to answer for if he does not seize the opportunity to achieve a degree of emancipation for the working classes, the oppressed, the insignificant. Oh, I know. The big men at the top will call me a demagogue. But, I don't care. If my conscience is clear . . .

DR. STOCKMANN: That's it, yes. That's it exactly, Mr. Hovstad. All the same. . . . Damn it. . . . (*a knock at the door*) Come in.

(*Aslaksen appears in the doorway. He is ordinarily dressed but decent, in black, with a white and somewhat crumpled cravat, gloves, and a top hat in his hand.*)

ASLAKSEN: (*bows*) I trust you'll forgive me for being so forward, Doctor.

DR. STOCKMANN: (*getting up*) Ah, good morning. You're Aslaksen, the printer, aren't you?

ASLAKSEN: I am indeed, Doctor.

HOVSTAD: (*getting up*) Are you looking for me, Aslaksen?

ASLAKSEN: No, I had no idea that I'd see you here. It was the Doctor I . . .

DR. STOCKMANN: Well, what can I do for you?

ASLAKSEN: Billing tells me that you're thinking of improving the water system. Is that true?

DR. STOCKMANN: Yes, for the baths.

ASLAKSEN: Ah, yes. Well, I just came to say that I'm with you all the way.

HOVSTAD: You see?

DR. STOCKMANN: I'm very grateful, but . . .

ASLAKSEN: You might find it a good thing to have us behind you, I mean, the tradesmen. We have quite a solid power base in this town when we choose to use it. And it's always good to have the majority behind you, Doctor.

DR. STOCKMANN: That's true. But, I don't see that there's any particular need at the moment. Surely this is all going to be pretty straightforward.

ASLAKSEN: Yes. But you might be happy to have us with you, all the same. I know the local authorities—the men in power don't like any interference from the outside. So I thought it would be a good idea if we organized a little demonstration.

HOVSTAD: That's what I think.

DR. STOCKMANN: A demonstration? What about? What sort of demonstration?

ASLAKSEN: It will be peaceful, Doctor. I always insist on peaceful demonstrations. Restraint is a primary necessity in civic matters, in my opinion anyway.

DR. STOCKMANN: Yes, yes, Mr. Aslaksen, your opinions are well known.

ASLAKSEN: Yes, I'm sure they are. Now, this problem with the water system is very important to us tradesmen. It looks as if the baths are going to be . . . you could say . . . a small gold mine for the town. All of us will be looking to the baths for our future livelihood, especially those of us who are property owners. That is why we want to support this project in every way possible. And, as I am chairman of the Property Owners Association . . .

DR. STOCKMANN: Yes.

ASLAKSEN: And as I am also secretary of the local Temperance Society. . . . You do know that I'm a member of the Temperance Society?

DR. STOCKMANN: Yes, yes.

ASLAKSEN: Well, it stands to reason that I come into contact with a lot of people, and since I'm known as a levelheaded, law-abiding citizen . . . it means . . . you said so yourself . . . it means I have some influence in the town. . . . I have a little power . . . if I do say so myself.

DR. STOCKMANN: I am well aware of that, Mr. Aslaksen.

ASLAKSEN: Yes. So . . . it would be easy for me to arrange a public testimonial if the opportunity should arise.

DR. STOCKMANN: A testimonial?

ASLAKSEN: Yes. Sort of a vote of thanks from our citizens to you for bringing this important matter to a successful end. Of course, we all realize that the tone has to be restrained. It mustn't offend the authorities and the . . . power brokers. If we're careful about that, no one can be offended, can they?

HOVSTAD: Well, even if they don't particularly like what's said, they . . .

ASLAKSEN: No, no, no. We mustn't offend the authority, Mr. Hovstad. We can't afford to take a stand against the very people upon whom our livelihood depends. I've seen that happen too often in my time. No good ever came of it. But the peaceful expression of liberal views can offend no one.

DR. STOCKMANN: (*shaking Aslaksen's hand*) My dear Aslaksen, I can't tell you how happy I am to find all this support from my fellow citizens. I am deeply touched, deeply touched. Well, now, how about a small glass of sherry?

ASLAKSEN: No, thank you. I never touch that kind of alcohol.

DR. STOCKMANN: A beer, then? Would you like one?

ASLAKSEN: No, thank you. Not that either, Doctor. I never touch a thing so early in the day. So, now I have to be getting back to town. I need to talk to some of the other property owners, start paving the way.

DR. STOCKMANN: That's really very kind of you, Mr. Aslaksen. But I really can't get it into my head that we need to be making all this fuss. My view is that it will all take care of itself.

ASLAKSEN: The authorities move somewhat slowly, Doctor. But God knows I don't intend to be criticizing them.

HOVSTAD: We'll give them a tongue-lashing in the paper tomorrow, Mr. Aslaksen.

ASLAKSEN: No violence, Mr. Hovstad. Restraint, restraint, restraint. Otherwise, we'll get nowhere with them. Trust me. I have become an expert in the school of life. Yes, well, I have to say goodbye. Now you know that we tradesmen stand behind you like a fortress, Doctor. You have the majority on your side, come what may.

DR. STOCKMANN: Thank you, my dear Mr. Aslaksen. (*shaking his hand*) Goodbye, goodbye.

ASLAKSEN: Are you coming down to the press, Mr. Hovstad?

HOVSTAD: I'll be there later. I've got a few things to do first.

ASLAKSEN: Yes, yes. (*bows and goes out; Dr. Stockmann goes with him*)

HOVSTAD: (*as the doctor comes back*) Well, what do you think of that, Doctor? Don't you think it's time we did a little shaking up of this complacency, this vacillation, this downright timidity?

DR. STOCKMANN: You mean Aslaksen?!

HOVSTAD: Yes. Oh, he's honest enough. But he's knee-deep in the swamp. And most of the other people are the same. They go this way and that way. They spend so much time looking at all sides of the question that they never make a move. At all.

DR. STOCKMANN: But Aslaksen seemed well intentioned, I thought.

HOVSTAD: There's something I think is much more important than that: to know your own mind and to have the courage of your convictions.

DR. STOCKMANN: Yes, you're right.

HOVSTAD: That's why I'm so anxious to seize this opportunity. I want to see if I can get these idiots, well-meaning idiots, to act like men for once. This groveling to authority has to stop. The mistakes they made over the water system are quite indefensible. That fact has to be drummed into the ears of every voting citizen.

DR. STOCKMANN: All right, if you think that's good for the community, go ahead. But I must talk with my brother first.

HOVSTAD: I'll write my editorial anyway. If the mayor refuses to take action, then . . .

DR. STOCKMANN: That's unthinkable.

HOVSTAD: It's possible. And if it happens?

DR. STOCKMANN: If it happens, I promise you that you can print my report. Yes, print the whole damned thing.

HOVSTAD: You promise?

DR. STOCKMANN: (*handing him the manuscript*) Here, take it with you. It won't do any harm if you read it. You can give it back to me later.

HOVSTAD: All right. I'll do that. Goodbye, Doctor.

DR. STOCKMANN: Goodbye, goodbye. Not to worry, Mr. Hovstad. Everything will go very smoothly, very smoothly.

HOVSTAD: Hmmm. We'll see.

(*Hovstad nods, goes out through the hallway. Dr. Stockmann goes to the dining room, looks in.*)

DR. STOCKMANN: Katherine!. . . oh, hello, Petra, you're back.

PETRA: (*enters*) He hasn't come yet?

DR. STOCKMANN: Peter? No. But I've had a long talk with Hovstad. He's very excited about my research. It seems it has greater significance than I thought. He's offered me his newspaper as a forum if I need it.

MRS. STOCKMANN: Do you think you will?

44

DR. STOCKMANN: No, I'm sure I won't. But it's good to know that you have the free press on your side, the mouthpiece of liberal views. Oh, and what do you think? I had a visit from the chairman of the Property Owners Association.

MRS. STOCKMANN: Oh? What did he want?

DR. STOCKMANN: He's on my side too. They're all on my side if there is any trouble. And Katherine, do you know what I have behind me?

MRS. STOCKMANN: Behind you? No. What do you have behind you?

DR. STOCKMANN: The solid majority.

MRS. STOCKMANN: I see. That's a good thing, is it?

DR. STOCKMANN: Of course it's a good thing. (*rubs his hands, walking up and down*) It's really good to feel that you stand side by side with your fellow citizens in a common bond.

PETRA: I just came back from school. You're doing such good and useful things, Father.

DR. STOCKMANN: Yes. And for the town too.

MRS. STOCKMANN: That's the doorbell.

DR. STOCKMANN: This must be him. (*a knock on the inner door*) Come in.

MAYOR: (*entering*) Good morning.

DR. STOCKMANN: (*warmly*) Hello, Peter.

MRS. STOCKMANN: Good morning. How are you?

MAYOR: Oh, thank you, pretty well. (*to the doctor*) Last night, long after office hours, I received a tract from you about the state of the water at the baths.

45

DR. STOCKMANN: Yes. Did you read it?

MAYOR: I did.

DR. STOCKMANN: Well? And what do you think?

MAYOR: (*looking at the others*) Hmmm.

MRS. STOCKMANN: Come with me, Petra. (*she and Petra go into the room on the left*)

MAYOR: (*after a pause*) Did you have to pursue all these investigations behind my back?

DR. STOCKMANN: Well, until I was absolutely certain . . . I . . .

MAYOR: And now you are?

DR. STOCKMANN: Yes. Surely you must see that I'm right.

MAYOR: Do you intend to place this document before the Baths Committee as an official complaint?

DR. STOCKMANN: Of course. Something has to be done quickly.

MAYOR: I find that your language in this document is somewhat extravagant. As usual. Among other things, you say that all we have to offer our visitors at the present time is a permanent state of ill health.

DR. STOCKMANN: Well, Peter, how else can you describe it? Just think. That water is toxic, even if you just bathe in it, let alone drink it. And we are offering this amenity to the unfortunate people who are sick, who have come to us in good faith, who are paying us good money. People who come here to get their health back.

MAYOR: And your conclusion is this: we must build a new sewage system to drain away the pollution

46

from the swamp at Moelledal . . . and the whole water system must be replaced.

DR. STOCKMANN: Is there another solution? I can't think of one.

MAYOR: This morning I went to see the town engineer. As we were talking I mentioned . . . half in jest . . . that your proposal might be a thing we could possibly undertake at some future date.

DR. STOCKMANN: Some future date?

MAYOR: He smiled. He clearly thought I was being excessive. I knew he would. Have you ever taken the time to think about how much this new construction would cost? I've talked to some people and the estimate is that it would probably run into several hundred thousands.

DR. STOCKMANN: That much?

MAYOR: Yes. But that's not the worst of it. It would take at least two years.

DR. STOCKMANN: Two years? Two whole years?

MAYOR: At least. And what do we do about the baths in the meantime? Shut them down? Yes, we'd have to. You think we'd get any visitors once it got out that the water was toxic?

DR. STOCKMANN: But, Peter, it is.

MAYOR: And for this to happen now! Just when the whole enterprise is on the verge of completion. There are other towns in the area which can justifiably be regarded as health spas. Don't you think they'll start trying to corner the market? Of course they will. And there we'll be. We'll have to abandon the whole thing . . . all that expense. You'll have ruined the town where you were born.

DR. STOCKMANN: Ruined?

MAYOR: The only future this town has is as a health resort, a spa. You must realize that as well as I do.

DR. STOCKMANN: Then what do you suggest we do?

MAYOR: I'm not completely convinced . . . from your report . . . that the situation is as dangerous as you are implying.

DR. STOCKMANN: Peter, if anything, it is worse, or at least it will be by the summer, once the hot weather comes.

MAYOR: As I said, I think you are exaggerating the danger. A professional medical officer must be able to take action. He must know how to prevent . . . any unpleasantness and then to cure it if it becomes an obvious problem.

DR. STOCKMANN: Carry on.

MAYOR: The water system that we have at the baths is a fact. It must be accepted as a fact. Nevertheless, in due time, I daresay that the committee might not be totally opposed to considering whether, if the financial considerations are not unreasonable, it might be possible . . . to contemplate some improvements.

DR. STOCKMANN: You think I'd let my name be attached to such a fraud?

MAYOR: A fraud?

DR. STOCKMANN: That's what it would be. A fraud, a lie, a crime against our community, against society as a whole.

MAYOR: I've already told you that I have not reached the point of convincing myself of any immediate or critical danger.

DR. STOCKMANN: Oh yes, you have. You must have. My reasoning, my evidence is irrefutable. I know that, and you know it too, Peter. But you won't admit it because it was you who forced the issue. It was you who made sure that the baths and the water pipes were placed where they are now. And you refused to admit that you made a huge blunder. Don't be a fool. Do you think I can't see right through you?

MAYOR: What if you are right? What if I am protective of my reputation? Of course I'm nervous. But I have the welfare of our town at heart. If I don't have moral authority, I cannot make decisions for the general good of the town in a way that I think is suitable. For this and many other reasons, it is vital to me that your paper not be placed before the Baths Committee. For the general good, it must be withheld. At a later date I'll bring it up for discussion, and we'll do the best we can. Discreetly. But nothing, not a single word, about this . . . unfortunate . . . matter must come before the public.

DR. STOCKMANN: Well, Peter, it can't be stopped now.

MAYOR: It must and will be stopped.

DR. STOCKMANN: It can't. Too many people already know.

MAYOR: Who knows? You mean those people from the *Tribune?*

DR. STOCKMANN: Oh yes. The free press of our country will make sure that you do your duty.

MAYOR: (*after a short pause*) You are a very foolish man, Thomas. Have you considered what the consequences of this might be for you?

DR. STOCKMANN: Consequences? For me?

49

MAYOR: Yes. For you and for your family.

DR. STOCKMANN: What the hell do you mean by that?

MAYOR: I think I've always been a good brother to you, whenever you've needed help.

DR. STOCKMANN: You have, and I'm grateful.

MAYOR: I'm not asking for thanks. To a certain extent . . . I've . . . been forced to do it . . . for my own sake. I always hoped I might be able to keep you in check if I could help your financial status.

DR. STOCKMANN: So, it was only to help yourself that you . . .

MAYOR: To some extent. It's very painful for a public servant to see his own brother compromising his life.

DR. STOCKMANN: You think I do that?

MAYOR: Unfortunately, yes. Without even knowing it. You are restless, aggressive, rebellious. And then there's this. You have this peculiar passion for rushing into print about every possible . . . every impossible . . . subject. The moment you get an idea, you have to sit down and write an article for the newspaper or a pamphlet about it.

DR. STOCKMANN: Look. If a man gets a new idea as a citizen, he has to make it public, doesn't he?

MAYOR: People don't like new ideas. People are comfortable with the good old ideas they've got already.

DR. STOCKMANN: You can say that to my face?

MAYOR: Yes. Thomas, I'm going to have to speak bluntly to you, for once. Till now I've avoided it because I know how headstrong you are. But now I have to tell you the truth. I don't think you realize how much you hurt yourself by being so impulsive. You constantly criticize the authorities, sometimes even the government. You vilify them, you claim you've been ostracized and persecuted. What else can you expect when you're such a difficult human being.

DR. STOCKMANN: So, I'm difficult too, am I?

MAYOR: Thomas, you are impossible to work with. I found that out for myself. You never think about anyone else's feelings. I think you even forget that it's me that you have to thank for getting you the job at the baths.

DR. STOCKMANN: I earned that. I was the first man to see that this town could prosper by establishing the baths. And at the time I was the only one to see that. I fought by myself for this project. For many years. I wrote and I wrote.

MAYOR: No one is denying that. But the time wasn't right then. Of course you didn't know that, isolated as you were up north in the woods, but as soon as the right time arrived, I and others joined the cause.

DR. STOCKMANN: Yes, and made a terrible mess of my wonderful idea. Oh yes, it's becoming very clear how brilliant all of you were.

MAYOR: In my opinion, all you are looking for now is another excuse for a fight. It's always the same. You have to pick a quarrel with those above you. That's been your fatal flaw. You can't stand having anyone in authority over you. You look down on anyone who has a position higher than yours. You think of him as a personal enemy.

51

And then it doesn't matter to you what form of attack you take. But now I've come clean. I've shown you what's at stake for the whole town and for me. I will not compromise.

DR. STOCKMANN: What do you mean?

MAYOR: You have been . . . indiscreet. You have discussed this delicate matter in public. It should have been kept a professional secret. Now, of course, the whole thing cannot be covered up. All kinds of rumors will begin to multiply. Those with a malicious bent in the town will feed these rumors. They will invent all kinds of "facts." It is therefore absolutely essential that you deny these rumors in public.

DR. STOCKMANN: I don't understand.

MAYOR: I am sure that once you consider the matter further, you will come to believe that this situation is not anywhere near as critical as you had first imagined.

DR. STOCKMANN: Aha. You're sure, are you?

MAYOR: Yes. I am also sure that you will express your confidence in the committee. In public. And announce your belief that the committee will take all necessary measures, conscientiously and in great detail, to remedy any possible defects.

DR. STOCKMANN: But you can't just patch things up. You can't solve this huge problem by simply ignoring it. Listen, Peter. Unless we start again from the very beginning I am absolutely sure that . . .

MAYOR: You're an employee. You have no right to be sure about anything independently.

DR. STOCKMANN: No right?

MAYOR: As an employee. You're a private individual
. . . well, God knows, that's something else. But as
a minor official at the baths you have no right to
express any public opinion that differs from that
of your immediate superiors.

DR. STOCKMANN: You are going too far. I am a doctor. I
am a man of science. I have no right?!

MAYOR: This is not merely a scientific matter. It is
much more complicated. The issues here involve
both technology and economics.

DR. STOCKMANN: I don't care how you frame the damn
thing; I have to be free to say what I think. About
anything.

MAYOR: Then go ahead. Just as long as it's not about
the baths. That is off-limits.

DR. STOCKMANN: (*shouting*) Off-limits? You . . . Look,
you're just a . . .

MAYOR: Yes. I am putting this off-limits. I am your em-
ployer, and when I say "no" to something, you
have to listen to me, obey me!

DR. STOCKMANN: (*trying to control himself*) Peter, if you
weren't my brother . . .

PETRA: (*opening the door*) Father, don't put up with
this!

MRS. STOCKMANN: (*following her in*) Petra, Petra.

MAYOR: Aha! We've got eavesdroppers.

MRS. STOCKMANN: You were talking so loud we
couldn't help hearing. . . .

PETRA: I was listening.

MAYOR: Well, I'm not completely sorry that . . .

DR. STOCKMANN: (*going toward him*) You said off-limits. You said I have to . . . obey you.

MAYOR: I was forced to use that tone.

DR. STOCKMANN: And you expect me to publicly deny what I believe in?

MAYOR: In our opinion, it is absolutely necessary that you issue a statement along the lines I have suggested.

DR. STOCKMANN: And if I don't . . . obey you?

MAYOR: Then we will be forced to issue our own explanation in order to keep the public peace.

DR. STOCKMANN: If you do, I shall write and counter your arguments. I will stick to my opinion. I will prove that I am right and you are wrong. What will you do then?

MAYOR: I will not have the power to prevent your being fired.

DR. STOCKMANN: What?

PETRA: Father, fired?

MRS. STOCKMANN: Fired?

MAYOR: Yes. You will be forced to leave your post as public medical officer. I will be forced to secure notice to be served on you immediately barring you from any further dealings with the baths.

DR. STOCKMANN: You have the arrogance to do that?

MAYOR: You're the one who's being arrogant.

PETRA: This is a disgraceful way to treat a man like my father.

MRS. STOCKMANN: Quiet, Petra.

MAYOR: (*looking at Petra*) So, you've got your own opinions too, have you? Of course. (*to Mrs. Stockmann*) Katherine, you seem to have the most sense in this house. Try to influence your husband in any way you can. He has to understand the consequences all this will have on his family and on . . .

DR. STOCKMANN: My family is of no concern to anyone but me.

MAYOR: . . . on his family and on the town he lives in.

DR. STOCKMANN: I am the one who has this town's real interests at heart. I will expose the harm that sooner or later will become public knowledge. I will prove to people that I love the town where I was born.

MAYOR: You can't see what you are doing. You're trying to destroy the source of the town's prosperity.

DR. STOCKMANN: That source is contaminated. This is insane. We make our living by selling filth and disease. And this "community" that you talk so much about is all based upon a lie.

MAYOR: That's just another flight of fancy . . . maybe worse. The man who slanders his own town in this way is an enemy of the people.

DR. STOCKMANN: (*going toward him*) You have the gall to . . .

MRS. STOCKMANN: (*coming between them*) Thomas.

PETRA: (*taking her father by the arm*) Calm down, Father.

MAYOR: I will not submit to violence. I've warned you. Consider your duty to yourself and to your family. Goodbye. (*leaves*)

DR. STOCKMANN: (*walking up and down*) In my own house! Katherine!

MRS. STOCKMANN: Yes, Thomas. It's shameful and it's scandalous.

PETRA: If I could get my hands on him . . .!

DR. STOCKMANN: It's all my own fault. I should have exposed them all a long time ago. I should have shown them my teeth and given them a good bite. To call me "an enemy of the people"—my God, I'm not going to take that lying down.

MRS. STOCKMANN: My dear Thomas, might is right.

DR. STOCKMANN: But I am the one who is right.

MRS. STOCKMANN: It's no good being right if the might is on the other side.

PETRA: Mother, how can you say that?

DR. STOCKMANN: So, in a free society, it means nothing to have right on one side? That's absurd, Katherine. And, isn't the free press standing before me? And isn't the solid majority standing behind me? Surely that's might enough.

MRS. STOCKMANN: Good heavens, Thomas, you can't really be thinking of picking a fight with your own brother?

DR. STOCKMANN: What the hell am I supposed to do? You don't want me to stand up for what I believe in?

PETRA: Yes, Father, you must.

MRS. STOCKMANN: It'll do no good. If they make up their minds, they'll make up their minds.

DR. STOCKMANN: (*laughing*) Katherine, just give me time. You'll see. I will fight this battle to the end.

MRS. STOCKMANN: Yes, you'll see. The end is going to be the loss of your job.

DR. STOCKMANN: At least I will have done my duty for the town, my duty to the people. They call me "an enemy of the people"?!

MRS. STOCKMANN: What about your family, Thomas? What about your home? Will you be doing your duty to those of us who depend on you?

PETRA: Mother, you mustn't think only of us.

MRS. STOCKMANN: That's easy for you to say. You can stand on your own two feet if you have to. But think of the boys, Thomas. Think of yourself, think of me.

DR. STOCKMANN: Katherine, that's insane. If I act like a coward, give in to Peter and his cronies, do you think I'll ever be happy again in my lifetime?

MRS. STOCKMANN: I don't know about that. But if the happiness in our future depends on you being so stubborn, God help us. We'll have no livelihood, no regular income. . . . Haven't we had enough of that all our lives? Think about that, Thomas. Think about what will happen.

DR. STOCKMANN: (*clenching his fists, fighting within himself*) And these bureaucrats? To do this to a free man, a man of honor? Isn't that a monstrous thing, Katherine?

MRS. STOCKMANN: Yes. They have treated you in the most wicked manner. True. But heaven knows, there is so much injustice in this world. What about the boys, Thomas? Think about them. What's going to happen to them? No. You can't find it in your heart to . . .

57

(Eilif and Morten enter with their schoolbooks)

DR. STOCKMANN: My boys. (*suddenly stands upright, having made up his mind*) Even if the whole world crashes down upon me, I will never bow my head. (*goes toward his room*)

MRS. STOCKMANN: Thomas, what are you going to do?

DR. STOCKMANN: (*in the doorway*) I must have the right to look into my sons' eyes when they are grown up, when they are free men. (*goes into his room*)

MRS. STOCKMANN: (*bursting into tears*) God help us.

PETRA: Father is right, Mother. And he'll never give in.

(The boys are bewildered. They ask what is wrong. Petra indicates to them to go.)

ACT 3

The editorial office of the Tribune. *On the left back wall is the entrance door. On the right is another door with windows through which the composing room can be seen. Another door is on the wall on the right. In the middle of the room is a large table covered with newspapers, other papers, and books. Downstage left is a window, with a writing desk and a high stool next to it. Two armchairs are at the table, and other chairs line the walls. The room is dark and uncomfortable. The furniture is old. The armchairs are dirty and worn. In the composing room a couple of typesetters are at work, and behind them a handpress is being used.*

Hovstad sits writing at the desk. A few moments later, Billing enters on the right with Dr. Stockmann's papers in hand.

BILLING: My God, my God, my God.

HOVSTAD: (*writing*) You've read it?

BILLING: (*putting the papers on the desk*) Yes I have, yes I have.

HOVSTAD: Pretty powerful, isn't it?

BILLING: Powerful? He'll slaughter them, by golly. Every paragraph is a knockout punch.

HOVSTAD: Those men won't fall to their knees after the first hit, though.

BILLING: True. But, we'll keep on slugging away, punch after punch, until this whole group of elitists collapses to the ground. When I was sitting there reading this, I thought I could see the revolution bursting into flames in the distance.

HOVSTAD: (*turning to him*) Shh! Don't let Aslaksen hear you.

BILLING: (*lowering his voice*) Aslaksen's a coward, a yellow-belly. He's not a man, he's got no guts. But, you're going to do it? You're going to publish the doctor's article?

HOVSTAD: Yes, unless the mayor backs off.

BILLING: That would be a damn nuisance.

HOVSTAD: Well, however it turns out, we can exploit the situation. If the mayor doesn't accept the doctor's proposal, all the tradesmen in town will turn on him . . . the Property Owners Association and the rest of them. If he does accept he'll turn all the big shareholders in the baths against him. They've been his main supporters up till now.

BILLING: Of course. They'll have to cough up a chunk of money.

HOVSTAD: You can bet on it. And the cabal will be crushed. Day after day, we'll bombard the public with the mayor's incompetence. I mean, in all kinds of ways. We'll take the view that all the important offices in the town, the whole municipal structure, ought to be handed over to people of the liberal persuasion.

BILLING: By golly, isn't that the truth! I can see it, I can see it. We're standing on the threshold of a revolution. (*a knock on the door*)

60

HOVSTAD: Shh. (*shouts*) Come in. (*Dr. Stockmann enters through the left door upstage, Hovstad goes toward him*) Ah. Here's the doctor. And?

DR. STOCKMANN: Roll the presses, Mr. Hovstad.

HOVSTAD: So, that's where we're at?

BILLING: Yippee!

DR. STOCKMANN: Roll the presses. Yes, that's where it's at. Well, now they will have what they want. It's war now, Mr. Billing.

BILLING: A war to the death, I hope. Let them have it, Doctor.

DR. STOCKMANN: This report is just the beginning. My brain is seething with ideas for oh, four or five other articles. Where's Aslaksen?

BILLING: (*calling into the composing room*) Aslaksen, come in here for a minute.

HOVSTAD: Four or five other articles, did you say? All on the same subject?

DR. STOCKMANN: No. . . . Good heavens, no, my dear man. No, they'll be about very different things. But, of course, it all has to do with this problem with the water system and the sewers. One thing leads to another, you know. It's just like when you begin to demolish an old building. Just like that.

BILLING: By golly, that's right. It's suddenly clear that you won't be done until you've demolished the whole dilapidated structure.

ASLAKSEN: (*from the composing room*) Demolished? Doctor, you're not thinking of pulling the baths down, are you?

HOVSTAD: No, no. Don't be alarmed.

61

DR. STOCKMANN: No, we were talking about something else. Well, Mr. Hovstad, what do you think of my report?

HOVSTAD: I think it's a masterpiece.

DR. STOCKMANN: You think so? That makes me very happy . . . very happy.

HOVSTAD: It's so clear, so . . . precise. And you don't have to be a specialist to follow your argument. I'm sure you'll have every clear-thinking person on your side.

ASLAKSEN: And every person of judgment too, I hope.

BILLING: Whether they can make judgments or not, you'll have the whole town behind you.

ASLAKSEN: Well, then, I don't think we have to be afraid of printing it.

DR. STOCKMANN: I damn well hope not.

HOVSTAD: It'll be in tomorrow's edition.

DR. STOCKMANN: Well, my God, yes. We can't afford to waste a single day. Oh, Mr. Aslaksen, there was something I wanted to ask you. I want you to take charge of this manuscript yourself.

ASLAKSEN: If you wish.

DR. STOCKMANN: Treat it like gold. No misprints, every single word is important. I'll drop by later. Perhaps you'll let me look at a proof? I can't tell you how anxious I am to see this thing in print. Hurled before the . . .

BILLING: Hurled, yes, like a bolt of lightning.

DR. STOCKMANN: And placed before the judgment of every intelligent citizen. You'll never guess what

62

I've had to put up with today. I've been threatened on all sides. They want to rob me of my basic rights as a human being. . . .

BILLING: Your basic human rights?

DR. STOCKMANN: They want to grind me into the dust, to turn me into a beggar. They are demanding that I place my own private interests above my most sacred and deeply held convictions.

BILLING: My golly, that's going too far.

HOVSTAD: That crowd will do anything.

DR. STOCKMANN: But they won't get very far with me. They'll get it in black and white. I'll battle with them every day in the *Tribune*. I'll fire one broadside after another.

ASLAKSEN: Yes, but you have to remember . . .

BILLING: Yippee, it's war, it's war.

DR. STOCKMANN: I'll beat them into the ground. I'll crush them. I'll break down their walls. Then every honest citizen will see. By God, I'm going to do it.

ASLAKSEN: But it has to be done . . . in a sober manner, Doctor, with restraint. . . .

BILLING: No, no. Don't spare the ammunition.

DR. STOCKMANN: (*imperturbable*) You see, it's not just the question of the water system and the sewers. The whole community has got to be . . . purified, decontaminated.

BILLING: . . . That's the exact word.

DR. STOCKMANN: We've got to get rid of all these men who think only of money and compromise. We

63

have to have a clean sweep. Oh, my eyes have been opened today. I look out on an endless landscape. I don't see how to get there yet, but I will. We need new standard-bearers, gentlemen. We need young men. The battlefront must be manned by a new army.

BILLING: Amen, amen.

DR. STOCKMANN: Just so long as we all stick together, it will be easy. Our revolution will be launched like a ship down a ramp. Am I right?

HOVSTAD: I think we have every prospect of getting the right man at the helm.

ASLAKSEN: But we must proceed with restraint. If we do, there's no danger.

DR. STOCKMANN: Danger? Who the hell cares? I am doing this for my conscience and for truth.

HOVSTAD: You deserve everyone's support, Doctor.

ASLAKSEN: Yes. The doctor is a true friend of this town, that's for sure. I'll go further. He's a friend of the people.

BILLING: By golly, Mr. Aslaksen, Dr. Stockmann is a true friend of the people.

ASLAKSEN: I think the Property Owners Association could use that phrase.

DR. STOCKMANN: (*moved and shaking their hands*) Thank you, my dear, my good friends, thank you. It does my soul good to hear this. My brother talked about me in very different terms. My God. I'll repay him and with interest. But now I have to go and see a patient, poor thing. But I'll be back. Take good care of the manuscript, Mr. Aslaksen, and for heaven's sake don't cut out any of the exclamation points. If anything, add a few. Good, good. Well, goodbye, goodbye, goodbye. (*shaking hands with them as they walk with him to the door*)

HOVSTAD: He's going to be god damned useful to us.

ASLAKSEN: As long as he just sticks to the baths. If he tries to go further, we'd be fools to stay with him.

HOVSTAD: Hmm. Well, that all depends. . . .

BILLING: Aslaksen, you're a damn coward.

ASLAKSEN: A coward? Yes I am, when it's a question of taking on the local authorities. That lesson I learned in the school of life. But see if I'm a coward if I enter a higher plane, national politics. Put me face-to-face with the government.

HOVSTAD: No, no, I'm sure you're not a coward. But, if I may say so, you're so inconsistent.

ASLAKSEN: That's because I know my duty as a citizen. You can't harm society if you attack the national government. It doesn't bother them, they just stay where they are. But local authorities are vulnerable. Throw them out and you may find inexperience at the helm. That would be disastrous for property owners and people like that.

HOVSTAD: But what about the issue of advancing the population through their experience in self-government?

ASLAKSEN: Where self-interest is involved, you can't think of everything, Mr. Hovstad.

HOVSTAD: Then I hope to God that I never have to think of my own self-interest.

BILLING: Amen.

HOVSTAD: I will never betray the people, never.

65

ASLAKSEN: In politics, Mr. Hovstad, you should never commit yourself. And you, Mr. Billing, if you want that job of clerk to the Council, you ought to trim your sails a bit.

BILLING: Me?

HOVSTAD: You, Billing?

BILLING: Well, I only applied for the job to annoy them, if you get my meaning.

ASLAKSEN: Well, it's none of my business, but since you called me a coward and inconsistent, I'd like to make one thing clear. My political record is open for anyone to see. I've never changed where I stand, apart from having learned to use more restraint. My heart is still with the people. But my head tells me to keep one eye on the authorities, the local ones anyway. (*goes into the composing room*)

BILLING: Couldn't we get another printer, Mr. Hovstad?

HOVSTAD: Do you know anyone else who'd give us credit, I mean for the printing and the paper?

BILLING: It's a damned nuisance not having any start-up capital.

HOVSTAD: (*sitting at desk*) Yes, that's exactly what we need.

BILLING: Ever thought about asking Dr. Stockmann?

HOVSTAD: (*shuffling through his papers*) What would be the use? He hasn't a dime.

BILLING: No, but he's got a good man behind him, old Morten Kiil, the man they call the Badger.

HOVSTAD: (*writing*) Do you really think he's got that much?

BILLING: By golly, of course he has, and some of it will go to the Stockmanns. He'll provide for, well, for the children anyway.

HOVSTAD: (*half turning*) You banking on that?

BILLING: Banking? I never bank on anything.

HOVSTAD: You'd better not. And don't bank on becoming the Council clerk, either, because, I can assure you, you won't.

BILLING: You think I don't know that? That's exactly what I want. Not to get it. An insult like that gets your dander up. You get a fresh supply of indignation. You need that in a one-horse town like this where nothing happens that really makes you angry.

HOVSTAD: (*writing*) Yes.

BILLING: Well, they'll soon be hearing from me. I'm going to ask for capital investment from the Property Owners Association.

(*Billing goes into the room on the right. Hovstad, sitting at desk chewing his pen, speaks slowly to himself.*)

HOVSTAD: Aha. So, that's what's up, is it? (*a knock at the door*) Come in!

(*Petra enters through the left door. Hovstad gets up.*)

HOVSTAD: Hello. What a surprise!

PETRA: I'm sorry to intrude. . . .

HOVSTAD: (*offering an armchair*) Please sit down.

PETRA: No, thank you, I can only stay for a moment.

HOVSTAD: Do you have something from your father?

PETRA: No, it's something from me. (*taking a book from her pocket*) Here's the English novel.

HOVSTAD: You're giving it back to me? Why?

PETRA: I don't want to translate it.

HOVSTAD: But you promised. . . .

PETRA: I hadn't read it then. And you can't have read it either.

HOVSTAD: No, you know I don't understand English, but . . .

PETRA: That's the point. That's why I wanted to tell you. . . . You'll have to find something else to print every week. (*puts the book on the table*) You can't possibly put this in the *Tribune*.

HOVSTAD: Why not?

PETRA: Because it is in fundamental opposition to what you believe in.

HOVSTAD: Is that the reason?

PETRA: I don't think you understand. Its central argument is that there is a supernatural power that looks after all the so-called "good" people of this world and that controls everything in such a way that in the end everything turns out well for them. . But all the so-called "bad" people are punished.

HOVSTAD: Yes. Well, that's all right . . . that's exactly what people want to read.

PETRA: But do you want to be the man who feeds them this stuff? You don't believe a word of it. You know very well that real life is not like that.

HOVSTAD: Of course it's not. But an editor doesn't always have the freedom to do as he wants. You have to make concessions to people's opinions . . . in unimportant matters. I mean, it's politics that are the most important thing . . . at least for a newspaper. And if my goal is to win the public over to my opinions about freedom and progress, then I mustn't scare them off. If they read a story on the back page with this kind of moral philosophy, they're more likely to agree with what we print on the front page. They feel comfortable.

PETRA: Oh, really! I don't believe you're as cunning as all that. I don't see you as some sort of spider spinning your web to catch your readers.

HOVSTAD: (*smiling*) Thank you for holding me in such high regard. Anyway, this was Billing's idea, not mine.

PETRA: Billing's?!

HOVSTAD: Yes. He was embracing those ideas here the other day. It was he who was so anxious to publish the novel. I'd never even heard of it.

PETRA: But Billing is a progressive.

HOVSTAD: Oh, there's more to Billing than what first meets the eye. I just heard that he's applied for the post of clerk to the Council.

PETRA: That's unbelievable, Mr. Hovstad! How could he find it within himself to do a thing like that?

HOVSTAD: You'd better ask him.

PETRA: I could never have imagined that Billing would . . .

HOVSTAD: You couldn't? Are you surprised?

PETRA: Yes. Maybe not, though. I don't really know.

HOVSTAD: We journalists are not a particularly honorable bunch, Miss Stockmann.

PETRA: How can you say that?

HOVSTAD: Well, sometimes that's what I think.

PETRA: As far as day-to-day things go, perhaps not. I can understand that. But right now, when you've taken on such an important cause . . .

HOVSTAD: You mean, your father?

PETRA: Yes. At this time you must feel that you are of more importance than most people.

HOVSTAD: Well, yes, I do feel a little bit that way today.

PETRA: It's true, isn't it? You really do. Think of the extraordinary vocation you've chosen. You can fight for truth. You can fight for new ideas. . . . In the face of neglect, you can stand before the world without fear and defend a man who's been wronged.

HOVSTAD: Especially when the man who's been wronged is . . . How can I put it?

PETRA: A man of such integrity and honor?

HOVSTAD: (*more quietly*) I was going to say, especially when he's your father.

PETRA: (*astonished*) Mr. Hovstad.

HOVSTAD: Yes, Petra . . . Miss Petra.

PETRA: Is that what you think is important? Not the issue itself? Not the truth? Not the fact that this means everything to my father?

HOVSTAD: Yes, yes, of course. All that too.

PETRA: No, thank you very much. You showed your real colors there, Mr. Hovstad. I will never believe you again, about anything.

HOVSTAD: Does it make you this angry that I've done all this for you?

PETRA: No. I'm angry because you haven't told my father the truth. You've been talking to him as though what mattered to you most was the truth . . . and the welfare of the people. You've made fools of both of us. You're not the man you pretend to be, and I'll never forgive you for that. Never.

HOVSTAD: You shouldn't be so harsh with me, Miss Petra, least of all just now.

PETRA: And why not now?

HOVSTAD: Because your father needs my help.

PETRA: So that's who you really are.

HOVSTAD: No, I didn't mean that . . . please believe me.

PETRA: I know what I believe. Goodbye.

ASLAKSEN: (*rushing in from the composing room*) For God's sake, Mr. Hovstad. (*sees Petra*) Oh, dear, that's unfortunate.

PETRA: There's the book. You can give it to somebody else. (*goes toward the door*)

HOVSTAD: (*going after her*) But Miss Petra.

PETRA: Goodbye. (*leaves*)

ASLAKSEN: Mr. Hovstad, listen to me, please.

HOVSTAD: Yes? What is it?

71

ASLAKSEN: The mayor is out there in the composing room.

HOVSTAD: The mayor?

ASLAKSEN: Yes. He wants to speak with you. He came in through the back door. . . . Didn't want to be seen, I guess.

HOVSTAD: What can he want? No, wait a minute. I'd better talk. . . . (*goes to the door of the composing room, opens it, bows, and asks the mayor to enter*) Keep an eye out, Aslaksen. Make sure no one . . .

ASLAKSEN: Of course. (*goes into the composing room*)

MAYOR: You didn't expect to see me here.

HOVSTAD: No, quite frankly, I didn't.

MAYOR: (*looking around*) You've done quite a nice job here, very nice.

HOVSTAD: Oh . . .

MAYOR: And here am I intruding, making demands on your time.

HOVSTAD: Not at all, sir. What can I do for you? (*taking the mayor's hat and walking stick, and putting them on a chair*) Allow me. . . . Won't you sit down?

MAYOR: (*sitting at the table*) Thank you. (*Hovstad also sits at the table*)

MAYOR: Mr. Hovstad, I've just had something extremely annoying happen to me today.

HOVSTAD: Really? Of course, Your Honor has so many responsibilities.

MAYOR: This particular matter concerns the medical officer at the baths.

HOVSTAD: Oh, the doctor?

MAYOR: He's written a . . . report to the Baths Committee. It concerns some possible defects in the baths.

HOVSTAD: That's amazing!

MAYOR: He hasn't told you? I thought he said . . .

HOVSTAD: Ah, yes. That's true. He did mention something.

ASLAKSEN: (*entering from the composing room*) I need that manuscript.

HOVSTAD: (*annoyed*) What? It's there on the desk.

ASLAKSEN: (*picking it up*) Good.

MAYOR: That must be it.

ASLAKSEN: Yes, this is the doctor's article, Your Honor.

HOVSTAD: Oh, is this what you were talking about?

MAYOR: Yes, it is. What do you think of it?

HOVSTAD: Of course, I'm not an expert, and I've only leafed through it.

MAYOR: But you are going to print it?

HOVSTAD: I can't very well refuse to publish an article that has a signature on it.

ASLAKSEN: Your Honor, I have no say in what we publish. . . .

MAYOR: Of course not.

ASLAKSEN: I just print what they give me.

MAYOR: Of course.

73

ASLAKSEN: So, if you'll excuse me . . . (*going toward the composing room*)

MAYOR: No, wait a minute, Mr. Aslaksen. With your permission, Mr. Hovstad?

HOVSTAD: Of course, Your Honor.

MAYOR: You're an intelligent man, Mr. Aslaksen. You have sound judgment.

ASLAKSEN: I'm glad Your Honor thinks so.

MAYOR: And you're a man of some importance in many circles in the town.

ASLAKSEN: Oh, they're mainly just ordinary people.

MAYOR: It's the small taxpayers who are in the majority, here and elsewhere.

ASLAKSEN: That's true.

MAYOR: And I am sure you know how most of them think, don't you?

ASLAKSEN: Yes, I think it's fair to say that I do, Your Honor.

MAYOR: Well, then. Since our less affluent citizens are prepared to make this sacrifice . . . and I praise them for it . . .

ASLAKSEN: What?

HOVSTAD: Sacrifice?

MAYOR: It's a wonderful example of civic duty, a really wonderful one. I was about to say that I hadn't expected it. But you know the mood of the public better than I do.

ASLAKSEN: But Your Honor . . .

74

MAYOR: And we can be sure that the sacrifice that the taxpayers will be asked to make will not be insignificant.

HOVSTAD: The taxpayers?

ASLAKSEN: I don't understand. . . . Surely, it's the shareholders . . .

MAYOR: This is a preliminary estimate, but the alterations that the medical officer thinks are necessary will cost between two and three hundred thousand crowns.

ASLAKSEN: That's a lot of money, but . . .

MAYOR: Of course we will have to raise a municipal loan.

HOVSTAD: (*getting up*) Surely you don't mean that the man in the street . . . ?

ASLAKSEN: You mean, you'd add it to the tax base? Take it out of the pockets of the tradesmen?

MAYOR: My dear Mr. Aslaksen, where else is the money to come from?

ASLAKSEN: That's a problem for the owners of the baths.

MAYOR: The committee does not see how they can authorize any further expenditure.

ASLAKSEN: And that's quite definite, Your Honor?

MAYOR: I have examined the problem in depth. If the people insist on these complete repairs, then the people themselves will have to pay for them.

ASLAKSEN: Almighty God. . . . I beg Your Honor's pardon. . . . This changes the situation entirely, Mr. Hovstad.

75

HOVSTAD: Indeed it does.

MAYOR: And worst of all is that we will have to close the baths for two or three years.

HOVSTAD: Close them? You mean completely?

ASLAKSEN: For two years?

MAYOR: Well, that's how long it will take, and that's the lowest estimate.

ASLAKSEN: Good heavens, Your Honor. We'll never be able to get through that. I mean, how are we property owners supposed to live in the meantime?

MAYOR: I'm afraid that's a difficult question to answer, Mr. Aslaksen. But what do you expect us to do? Do you think we will get one single visitor here if we start telling people that the water is polluted? That we are living over a cesspool? That the whole town . . .

ASLAKSEN: And this is just a theory?

MAYOR: I have tried very hard, but I have not been able to convince myself that it is anything but a theory.

ASLAKSEN: But, if that's the case, it is unforgivable of Dr. Stockmann to have . . . I beg your pardon, Your Honor, but . . .

MAYOR: I hate to agree with your comment, Mr. Aslaksen, but I'm afraid it is the truth. Unfortunately, my brother has always been . . . impulsive.

ASLAKSEN: And you still stand behind him in all this, Mr. Hovstad?

HOVSTAD: Who could possibly have thought that . . . ?

MAYOR: I have written a brief synopsis of the problem as it appears to . . . an impartial observer. In it I have made suggestions of how any potential flaws in the current system could be corrected, safely, within the current financial resources of the baths.

HOVSTAD: Do you have that document with you, Your Honor?

MAYOR: (*tapping his pocket*) Yes. I brought it with me, just in case.

ASLAKSEN: (*quickly*) Oh good heavens, here he is.

MAYOR: Who, my brother?

HOVSTAD: Where, where?

ASLAKSEN: He's just coming through the composing room.

MAYOR: That's most unfortunate. I don't want him to see me here. And I've got something else I wanted to talk to you about.

HOVSTAD: (*pointing to the door on the right*) Go in there until he's gone.

MAYOR: But?

HOVSTAD: Only Billing is in there.

ASLAKSEN: Quick, quick, Your Honor. He's coming.

MAYOR: All right, but get rid of him as soon as you can. (*goes out the door, which Aslaksen opens for him*)

HOVSTAD: Find something to do, Aslaksen. (*Hovstad sits down and writes. Aslaksen looks through a pile of newspapers on a chair.*)

DR. STOCKMANN: (*entering from the composing room*) Well, I'm back. (*puts down his hat and walking stick*)

HOVSTAD: (*writing*) So soon, Doctor?

ASLAKSEN: Hurry up with what we were talking about. We're really behind today.

DR. STOCKMANN: (*to Aslaksen*) You don't have the proofs yet, I gather?

ASLAKSEN: (*not looking up*) No. You didn't think they'd be ready yet?

DR. STOCKMANN: That's all right. I'm sure you understand. I'm just impatient. I can't sit still till I've seen that thing in print.

HOVSTAD: It'll be some time yet, won't it, Aslaksen?

ASLAKSEN: I'm afraid so.

DR. STOCKMANN: All right, my dear friends, I'll come back later. I don't mind coming back twice, if necessary. In a matter of such importance . . . I mean, the welfare of the whole town is at stake—you have to make a little extra effort. (*about to leave, but stops and comes back*) Oh, by the way, there's one more thing I must talk to you about.

HOVSTAD: Sorry. Couldn't you wait until later?

DR. STOCKMANN: I can tell you in a couple of words. It's just this. . . . When people read my article tomorrow and realize that I've been racking my brains all winter long, working hard for the welfare of the town . . .

HOVSTAD: But Doctor.

DR. STOCKMANN: I know what you're thinking. You think I was just doing my damn duty . . . being a good citizen. Yes, that's right. I know that as well as you. But my fellow citizens . . . you see . . . those good people . . . they admire me.

ASLAKSEN: Yes. The people here have indeed admired you, Doctor, until today.

DR. STOCKMANN: And that's why I'm frightened . . . I mean . . . when they read this, especially the poor people . . . when they see this as a wake-up call, telling them to take the government of their own town into their own hands . . .

HOVSTAD: (*getting up*) Look, Doctor, I don't want to keep anything from you. . . .

DR. STOCKMANN: Aha. Something's already being planned. I could have guessed. I don't want it. I don't want any public recognition.

HOVSTAD: Like what?

DR. STOCKMANN: Well, if people are thinking of a parade, or a banquet, or getting me some little token of appreciation, you must promise me that you'll put an end to it. And you too, Mr. Aslaksen, you hear?

HOVSTAD: I'm sorry, Doctor, but we might as well tell you the truth right now. . . . (*Mrs. Stockmann, in hat and cloak, enters through the left door*)

MRS. STOCKMANN: (*seeing the doctor*) I knew it.

HOVSTAD: (*going toward her*) You're here too, Mrs. Stockmann?

DR. STOCKMANN: What the hell are you doing here, Katherine?

MRS. STOCKMANN: Surely you can guess.

HOVSTAD: Won't you have a seat, or perhaps . . . ?

MRS. STOCKMANN: Thank you, don't trouble yourself, and please don't be offended that I came here to get my husband. I'm the mother of his three children, you know.

DR. STOCKMANN: Oh, really, Katherine. We all know . . .

MRS. STOCKMANN: Well, it doesn't look as if you've been thinking about your wife and children or you wouldn't have come here and made us all so miserable.

DR. STOCKMANN: That's so irrational, Katherine. Just because a man has a wife and children, is he not allowed to tell the truth . . . to be a useful and productive citizen . . . to serve the town he lives in?

MRS. STOCKMANN: Oh, Thomas, just use some restraint.

ASLAKSEN: That's just what I say, restraint in everything.

MRS. STOCKMANN: And as for you, Mr. Hovstad, it is not right for you to influence my husband like this . . . to make him leave his house and home . . . to fool him into getting involved in all of this.

HOVSTAD: I haven't fooled anyone.

DR. STOCKMANN: Fooled? You think I allow myself to be fooled?

MRS. STOCKMANN: Yes. Oh, I know, you're about the cleverest man in town, but it's so easy to fool you, Thomas. (*to Hovstad*) And remember that he will lose his job at the baths if you print what he's written.

ASLAKSEN: What?!

HOVSTAD: Doctor, I uh, I uh, I . . .

DR. STOCKMANN: (*laughing*) Just let them try. Oh no, Katherine, they'll be careful. I have the majority behind me.

MRS. STOCKMANN: Yes, that's the problem. That's a dangerous thing to have behind you.

DR. STOCKMANN: Nonsense, Katherine. Go home now and take care of the house. Let me take care of society. How can you be afraid when I feel so calm, so happy? (*rubbing his hands and walking up and down*) Truth will win. The people will win. You have nothing to be afraid of. I can see it now. Every freethinking citizen on the march . . . an army that can't be defeated. (*stops by a chair*) What the hell is this?

ASLAKSEN: (*looking at it*) Oh, dear!

DR. STOCKMANN: The king's crown! (*taking the mayor's hat in his hands and holding it in the air*)

MRS. STOCKMANN: The mayor's hat.

DR. STOCKMANN: And his scepter of office too. What in the name of hell?

HOVSTAD: Well . . .

DR. STOCKMANN: I see. He's been here to win you over. (*laughing*) He came to the wrong place. And then, he saw me in the composing room. . . . (*roaring with laughter*) Did he run away, Mr. Aslaksen?

ASLAKSEN: (*quickly*) Yes, Doctor, he ran away.

DR. STOCKMANN: Ran away without his stick and his . . . Nonsense! Peter never left anything behind in his life. But where the hell have you put him? Ah, yes, of course, in there. Now, Katherine, watch this.

MRS. STOCKMANN: Thomas, please!

ASLAKSEN: Don't do anything stupid, Doctor.

(*Dr. Stockmann puts the hat on his head and takes the stick. He crosses the room, opens the door, brings his*

81

hand up to the hat in salute. The mayor enters, flushed with anger. Billing follows.)

MAYOR: What is the meaning of all this?

DR. STOCKMANN: Show me a little more respect, please, my dear Peter. I am the king of the town now. (*paces around*)

MRS. STOCKMANN: (*almost in tears*) Thomas, please.

MAYOR: (*following him*) Give me my hat and stick.

DR. STOCKMANN: You may be the police chief, but I am the mayor. I am in charge of this whole town. Oh yes!

MAYOR: Take off that hat. Remember that it is an official symbol of . . .

DR. STOCKMANN: Nonsense. Do you think that the newly awakened lion of public opinion is going to be frightened of a hat? Tomorrow the revolution starts, I'll have you know. You threatened to fire me. But now it's I who will fire you . . . fire you from all your positions of power. You think I can't? Then you're wrong, Peter. I have an army beside me . . . the unbeatable army of social revolution. Hovstad and Billing will make thunder in the *Tribune.* Mr. Aslaksen will march at the head of the Property Owners Association.

ASLAKSEN: No, Doctor, I will not.

DR. STOCKMANN: Yes, you will.

MAYOR: Aha! Perhaps Mr. Hovstad will be behind this revolution.

HOVSTAD: No, Your Honor.

ASLAKSEN: Mr. Hovstad is no fool. He's not going to ruin himself and his newspaper for the sake of a . . . figment of someone's imagination.

DR. STOCKMANN: (*looking around*) What the hell?

HOVSTAD: The case you have made is false, Doctor, therefore I cannot support you.

BILLING: No. After what His Honor was kind enough to tell me in there, I wouldn't. . . .

DR. STOCKMANN: All lies! I'll stand behind the truth of my report. You print it, I'll defend it. I'm not afraid.

HOVSTAD: I'm not going to print it. I can't, I won't, I dare not print it.

DR. STOCKMANN: Dare not? What nonsense. You're the editor, and the editor controls the press.

ASLAKSEN: No, Doctor, it's the subscribers.

MAYOR: Fortunately.

ASLAKSEN: It's public opinion, it's the educated reader, it's the property owners, and so on—they control the press.

DR. STOCKMANN: (*calmly*) And these are the forces that are set up against me?

ASLAKSEN: They are. If your report were printed, the whole community would be ruined.

DR. STOCKMANN: I see.

MAYOR: My hat and stick. (*Dr. Stockmann takes off the hat and puts it and the stick on the table*)

MAYOR: (*picking them up*) Your little kingdom didn't last long.

DR. STOCKMANN: It's not over yet. (*to Hovstad*) I take it you are refusing, absolutely, to print my report in the *Tribune*?

HOVSTAD: Absolutely, if only for the sake of your family.

83

MRS. STOCKMANN: His family is of no concern of yours, Mr. Hovstad.

MAYOR: (*taking papers from his pocket*) This will give the public all the necessary facts. It's an official statement. Mr. Hovstad . . . ?

HOVSTAD: (*taking the paper*) Right. I'll set it up at once.

DR. STOCKMANN: And what about mine? You think you can put a gag in my mouth, stifle the truth? It's not going to be that easy. Mr. Aslaksen, take my manuscript and print it immediately. Print a pamphlet at my own expense. I'll be the publisher. I want four hundred copies . . . five hundred . . . no, six hundred copies.

ASLAKSEN: I wouldn't allow you to use my press if you offered me gold, Doctor. I dare not. Public opinion wouldn't allow it. You won't find a printer for it anywhere in town.

DR. STOCKMANN: Give it back to me, then. (*Hovstad hands him the manuscript*)

DR. STOCKMANN: (*taking his hat and stick*) I'll make sure the contents are made known all the same. I'll call a public meeting and read it aloud. All my fellow citizens must know the truth.

MAYOR: You won't find anyone here who will lease you a space. . . .

ASLAKSEN: No one. I'm sure of that.

BILLING: By golly, no you won't find anyone. . . .

MRS. STOCKMANN: This is disgraceful. Why are they all turning against you?

DR. STOCKMANN: (*in anger*) I'll tell you why. In this town all the men are old women. Just like you, they think only of their families and not of society.

84

MRS. STOCKMANN: (*grasping his arm*) Then I'll show them. An old woman can be a man; I'm standing beside you, Thomas.

DR. STOCKMANN: Well said, Katherine. The truth must be told, and by God it will! If I can't rent a space, I'll hire a drummer to march through the town with me, and I'll read my report on every street corner.

MAYOR: You can't be that insane.

DR. STOCKMANN: Oh yes I can.

ASLAKSEN: You won't find a single citizen who'll march with you.

BILLING: No, by golly.

MRS. STOCKMANN: Don't give in, Thomas. I'll ask the boys to march with you.

DR. STOCKMANN: That's a great idea.

MRS. STOCKMANN: Morten will love it and so will Eilif, I'm sure.

DR. STOCKMANN: Yes, and Petra too. And you, Katherine.

MRS. STOCKMANN: No, no, not me. But I'll stand in the window and watch you, I will, I will.

DR. STOCKMANN: (*throwing his arms around her and kissing her*) Thank you. Well, gentlemen, let the trumpets sound. We'll see whether mediocrity and cowardice have the power to silence a man who wants to clean up society. (*Dr. and Mrs. Stockmann leave through the left door*)

MAYOR: (*shaking his head*) Now he's driven her insane too.

85

ACT 4

A large, old-fashioned room in Captain Horster's house. An open double-door leading to a lobby is at the back of the room. On the left wall are three windows. A dais has been placed in the center of the opposite wall. On it is a small table with two candles, a carafe of water, a glass, and a bell. The room is lit by lamps on the walls between the windows. Down left are a table with a candle on it, and a chair. Down right are a door and a few chairs.

A large crowd of citizens of all classes is gathered, including a few women and a few schoolboys. More and more people come in from the back, filling the room.

A CITIZEN: (*to someone he bumps into*) Hello, Lamstad, you here too?

SECOND CITIZEN: I never miss a public meeting.

THIRD CITIZEN: (*approaching them*) Brought your whistle, I hope?

SECOND CITIZEN: Of course I have, have you?

THIRD CITIZEN: You betcha. Captain Evensen said he was going to bring a damn big horn.

SECOND CITIZEN: He's a riot, old Evensen is. (*laughter*)

FOURTH CITIZEN: (*joining them*) Tell me, what's this meeting all about?

86

SECOND CITIZEN: Dr. Stockmann is going to give a lecture. He's going to attack the mayor.

FOURTH CITIZEN: The mayor's his brother.

FIRST CITIZEN: Don't matter a bit. Dr. Stockmann don't fear nobody.

THIRD CITIZEN: But he's all wrong. It said so in the *Tribune.*

SECOND CITIZEN: Yep. He must be wrong this time. The property owners wouldn't let him use their hall, nor the people's club too.

FIRST CITIZEN: He couldn't even get the hall at the baths.

SECOND CITIZEN: Well, what do you expect?

FIRST CITIZEN: Who do you think we ought to support?

FOURTH CITIZEN: Keep an eye on Aslaksen. Do what he does.

BILLING: (*carrying papers under his arm and pushing his way through the crowd*) 'Scuse me, 'scuse me. I have to report for the *Tribune.* Thank you. (*sitting down at the table on the left*)

A WORKER: Who was that?

ANOTHER WORKER: You don't recognize him? It's that guy Billing who works for Aslaksen's paper.

(*Captain Horster comes in with Mrs. Stockmann and Petra through the right door. Eilif and Morten come too.*)

HORSTER: I thought you should sit here. You can get out quickly if anything happens.

MRS. STOCKMANN: Do you think there's going to be trouble?

HORSTER: You never know with a crowd like this. But sit down and don't worry.

MRS. STOCKMANN: (*sits*) It was very kind of you to offer my husband this room.

HORSTER: Well, no one else would, so I . . .

PETRA: (*sitting*) It was very brave of you, Captain Horster.

HORSTER: Oh, it didn't take much courage.

(*Hovstad and Aslaksen enter separately*)

ASLAKSEN: (*going over to Horster*) The doctor isn't here yet?

HORSTER: He's waiting in there.

(*a noise among the crowd, near the back door*)

HOVSTAD: (*to Billing*) There's the mayor. See?

BILLING: Yes, by golly, so he's come after all.

(*The mayor enters, pushes his way through the crowd, greets people, and stands against the wall on the left. Soon Dr. Stockmann enters through the door on the right. He is wearing a black frockcoat and a white cravat. A few people clap, but there is also a quiet hissing. It grows silent.*)

DR. STOCKMANN: (*quietly*) How are you feeling, Katherine?

MRS. STOCKMANN: I'm all right. (*even more quietly*) Don't lose your temper, Thomas.

DR. STOCKMANN: Oh, I'll watch myself, don't worry. (*looks at his watch, steps to the dais, and bows*) It's fifteen after, so I'll begin. (*takes out his manuscript*)

ASLAKSEN: Shouldn't we elect a chairman first?

DR. STOCKMANN: No, no. It's not necessary.

(*Several people shout*) Yes, yes.

MAYOR: I really think we should have a chair.

DR. STOCKMANN: Peter, I called this meeting to give a lecture.

MAYOR: But the doctor's lecture might very well provoke very different opinions.

(*Several people shout*) A chair, a chairman.

HOVSTAD: The public seems to want a chairman.

DR. STOCKMANN: (*controlling himself*) Very well, let the public have its way.

ASLAKSEN: Would His Honor, the Mayor, be willing to take the chair?

(*Several people clap and shout*) Yes, yes! Bravo!

MAYOR: I must decline . . . for reasons which I'm sure you all understand. Fortunately, however, we have here with us this evening a man who I think is acceptable to all of us. I mean, of course, the chairman of the Property Owners Association, Mr. Aslaksen.

(*Several people shout*) Yes, yes, Aslaksen! Aslaksen!

(*Dr. Stockmann picks up his manuscript and leaves the dais*)

ASLAKSEN: If my fellow citizens wish to put their trust in me, I won't refuse them.

(*Several people clap and cheer. Aslaksen steps up onto the dais.*)

BILLING: (*writing*) Mr. Aslaksen was selected amidst general acclamation. . . .

ASLAKSEN: Since I am standing here, may I beg your permission to say a few words? I am a quiet man, a peaceful man. I believe in moderate caution and . . . and . . . cautious moderation. Everyone who knows me will avouch that.

THE CROWD: (*variously*) That's true! . . . You're right there, Aslaksen!

ASLAKSEN: I have learned this in the school of life. Experience has taught me that restraint is the most important virtue that a citizen can possess. . . .

MAYOR: Amen! Amen!

ASLAKSEN: Moderation and caution are the cornerstones of society. I would therefore suggest to our esteemed fellow citizen, who has called this meeting, that he do his utmost to stay within the bounds of moderation.

DRUNKEN MAN BY THE DOOR: Up with the Temperance Society! Cheers! Here's to you!

A CITIZEN: Shut up!

CITIZENS: Shh! Shh!

ASLAKSEN: Gentlemen, please! No interruptions! Now does anyone wish to say anything before I . . . ?

MAYOR: Mr. Chairman!

ASLAKSEN: Your Honor?

MAYOR: As you are all aware, I have a close relationship with the current medical officer at the baths, and, consequently, I would have preferred not to speak this evening. However, I have an official position on the Baths Committee. And I possess a deep solicitude for the well-being of our town. Therefore I feel compelled to table a motion.

I venture to presume that no citizen here with us tonight would consider it desirable that unsubstantiated and exaggerated allegations concerning the sanitary conditions at the baths might circulate outside our town.

CITIZENS: No! No! No! Absolutely not! It shouldn't happen!

MAYOR: I therefore move that this body refuse permission for the medical officer either to read . . . or to comment on . . . his proposed lecture.

DR. STOCKMANN: Refuse permission? What the hell?

(*Mrs. Stockmann coughs*)

DR. STOCKMANN: (*composing himself*) All right. So you refuse permission?

MAYOR: I made a statement, published in the *Tribune.* In it I spelled out the central facts in this case. And now every intelligent citizen can make his own judgment. I spoke of many things, but I pointed out that our medical officer's proposals . . . quite apart from the fact that they are no more than a vote of no confidence in our leading citizens . . . are in effect a proposed burden on our taxpayers . . . an unnecessary burden I may add . . . of at least a hundred thousand crowns.

(*Crowd reacts. Aslaksen silences them with his bell.*)

ASLAKSEN: Order! Order! Gentlemen, please! I wish to second Your Honor's motion. Furthermore, it is clear to me that the doctor has had an ulterior motive in all of this. Unconscious maybe, but a motive that seeks to disrupt our society. He talks specifically about the baths, but he is in fact seeking turmoil and revolution. He seeks change, the transference of authority. The doctor is an honest man. We all know that, God knows. I myself believe in government by the people, deeply. But it must not impose an excessive burden on the taxpayer. But that is just what is happening here. And I'll be damned . . . if you'll pardon the expression . . . if I will support Dr. Stockmann in this matter. You can pay too much for principle. That's my opinion.

(*crowd reacts with essential agreement*)

HOVSTAD: I too must add my thoughts. At first Dr. Stockmann's position, indeed his passion, won him considerable sympathy. I myself was on his side. Impartial of course. But then we found out that we had been misled. The facts were not facts. . . .

DR. STOCKMANN: That is a lie!

HOVSTAD: Not completely reliable then. His Honor's statement has shown that. I am a liberal. The *Tribune* reflects our position on major political issues. You all know that. But my experience and my conversations with men of . . . discretion and experience . . . have taught me to be cautious over . . . certain . . . matters.

ASLAKSEN: Those are exactly my feelings.

HOVSTAD: So let's get back to the matter we are discussing here. . . . Dr. Stockmann has popular opinion against him. That's clear. So I ask you, what is an editor's function? Is it not to give a mirror image of his readers' thoughts? Is he not given the right—we might call it an unspoken mandate—to promote the views of those readers who share his own? And with eloquence. Am I wrong?

CROWD: We agree!

HOVSTAD: It has been difficult. It has broken my heart. . . . I have eaten at his house. Often, and recently too. To break ranks with him is hard. . . . You see, until this moment in time he has enjoyed the universal affection of his fellow citizens. . . . His only, or let's say principal, fault has been that he follows his heart rather than his head.

(*general approbation*)

HOVSTAD: But I have a duty to the society in which I live. And I have no choice. And there is one thing more which forces me to stand against him— because I hope that I can reverse the path that he has chosen—it is this . . . the effect on his family.

DR. STOCKMANN: Talk about the water system and the sewers!

HOVSTAD: The effect on his wife and the children he has abandoned!

MORTEN: Us, Mother?

MRS. STOCKMANN: Shh.

ASLAKSEN: I will now put His Honor's proposition to the vote.

DR. STOCKMANN: Don't bother. I won't even mention those damned baths. I have something else to say tonight. . . .

MAYOR: (*quietly*) What the devil is this?

THE DRUNK: (*at the door*) I pay my taxes! I can tell you what I think! And it's my absolute and in . . . in . . . comprehensible opinion that . . .

CROWD: Throw him out!

(*he is removed*)

DR. STOCKMANN: Do I have the floor?

ASLAKSEN: (*rings the bell*) Dr. Stockmann has the floor.

DR. STOCKMANN: Just a few days ago, if anyone had tried to silence me like this, I'd have fought like a lion for my basic rights as a human being. But now all that means nothing. Now I have more important things on my mind.

(*The crowd moves in closer. Morten Kiil is seen among them.*)

DR. STOCKMANN: I have been thinking a great deal these past few days, deeply . . . thinking so much that my head was ready to explode. . . .

(*the mayor coughs*)

DR. STOCKMANN: But then everything began to fall into place. I saw everything with perfect clarity. And that is why I am here before you tonight. I have something very important to say to you, my friends. I saw it all with sudden lucidity. And the revelation is this: I have discovered something infinitely more important than the piddling fact that our water system is polluted and that our health spa sits above a cesspool.

CROWD: Don't talk about the baths! Leave them alone! We won't hear that stuff!

DR. STOCKMANN: What I have discovered in these last few days—and this is infinitely more important—is that our *spiritual* springs are toxic . . . and that the whole social system, which we prize so much, also sits above a cesspool.

VOICES: What? What did he say?

MAYOR: This is ridiculous. . . .

ASLAKSEN: (*holding the bell aloft*) I must request that the speaker moderate his language!

DR. STOCKMANN: I have loved this place where I was born, loved it like no other. It was where I spent my youth. When I left home I was still young. And living away from here, what with the longing for home, my memory shed a warm light on this place and the people who live here.

(*some sporadic cheers*)

DR. STOCKMANN: For many years I lived in a hellhole up north. As I lived and worked among those people of the mountains, I often thought that those backward creatures would have been better off with a vet, not a doctor.

(*the crowd murmurs*)

BILLING: (*putting down his pen*) By golly, I've never heard anything like that. . . .

HOVSTAD: That's foul slander against a respectable community!

DR. STOCKMANN: Hold on! No one can accuse me of forgetting the place of my birth. I sat up there like a duck on an egg, brooding, and the plan that I hatched was the Municipal Baths.

(*some clapping, some sounds of disapproval*)

DR. STOCKMANN: (*continuing*) Then, at long last, fate decreed that I should come home. Ah then, ah then, my fellow citizens, I felt there was nothing left for me to wish for. No—I had one burning constant desire—to be of service to my native town and this community.

95

MAYOR: (*gazing out into space*) You have a strange way of showing it.

DR. STOCKMANN: I spent my days in the sheer blind joy of my newfound happiness, but yesterday morning . . . no, in fact, it was the previous night, my eyes were opened. And when I opened them, the first thing I saw was the enormous stupidity of the authorities.

(*Shouting and laughter, lots of noise. Mrs. Stockmann coughs loudly.*)

MAYOR: Mr. Chairman!

ASLAKSEN: (*ringing his bell*) As chairman of this meeting, I . . .

DR. STOCKMANN: Oh, let's not quibble about a few words, Mr. Aslaksen. All I meant was that I suddenly realized that our politicians had behaved shamelessly down there at the baths. I hate politicians. I never want to see another one. They're like a herd of goats in a tree farm. They eat up everything. They stand in the path of a free man, whichever way he wants to turn. I'd like to see them exterminated like any other vermin.

(*a loud noise in the hallway*)

MAYOR: Mr. Chairman, can we allow such slanderous . . . ?

ASLAKSEN: (*holding the bell*) Dr. Stockmann!

DR. STOCKMANN: I don't understand why I never saw these gentlemen with clear eyes before. I mean, I had a perfect example in front of me all this time—my brother, Peter, a slow-witted lump of hypocrisy.

(*Laughter, whistling, and mass confusion. Mrs. Stockmann coughs loudly. Aslaksen rings his bell.*)

96

THE DRUNK: (*returns*) Are you talking about me? My name's Petersen, and don't you damn well . . .

CROWD: Throw the drunk out! Get him out of here. (*the drunk is thrown out*)

MAYOR: Who was that?

BYSTANDERS: I don't know, Your Honor. He's not from around here. He's some day laborer.

ASLAKSEN: He was clearly intoxicated . . . too much beer. You may go on, Doctor, but please try to moderate your tone.

DR. STOCKMANN: Well, my fellow citizens, I won't talk about politicians anymore. If any of you think I came here this evening to attack these gentlemen, you'd be wrong. Quite wrong. You see, I have a deeply held belief . . . and it is a comforting one . . . that these parasites . . . these relics of a dying world are inexorably destroying themselves. They don't need a doctor to help them finish the job. And anyway, they're not the main danger to society. They aren't the men who are principally responsible for poisoning our spiritual life and contaminating the ground on which we walk. They are not the most dangerous enemies of truth and freedom in this society.

BYSTANDERS: Who, then? Name names.

DR. STOCKMANN: Oh, I'll name names, don't you worry, because this is the great discovery that I made yesterday. (*raising his voice*) The most dangerous enemy of truth and freedom is the so-called solid majority. Yes. The damned liberal majority. Those are the people we have to fear. So, now you know.

(*Complete uproar. Everyone is shouting, stamping their feet, and whistling. Some members of the audience look*

97

at each other and seem to be enjoying it all. Mrs. Stockmann stands up nervously. Eilif and Morten go over to the schoolboys and threaten them. Aslaksen rings his bell and calls for silence. Hovstad and Billing talk to each other. Finally there is silence.)

ASLAKSEN: As chairman, I call upon the speaker to retract those appalling remarks.

DR. STOCKMANN: Never, Mr. Aslaksen. It's the majority in this community that is denying me my freedom and is trying to stifle the truth.

HOVSTAD: The majority is always right.

BILLING: And, by golly, tells the truth.

DR. STOCKMANN: The majority is never right! Never. Never! That's one of the lies that is bred in this community, and freethinking men have to fight against it. Who is this majority . . . in any country? Is it the wise or the fools? I think we all have to admit that the fools form the overwhelming majority throughout this world. And it's terrifying. But, in God's name, how can it be right that fools hold sway over the wise?

(*shouting and uproar*)

DR. STOCKMANN: Oh yes, you can try to shout me down, but you can't deny that I am right. The majority rules—that's true, unfortunately—but the majority is not right. The people who are right are a few rare individuals like me. The minority is always right.

(*renewed shouting*)

HOVSTAD: So, Dr. Stockmann has become an aristocrat in just a couple of days.

DR. STOCKMANN: I've already told you that I don't want to waste my words on the mindless mob huffing and puffing along behind us. Real life brings them no excitement. I'm talking about the few rare individuals in our midst who live by new and vital truths. These are the men who stand in the vanguard, in the outposts of our society. The majority is left far behind. These are the men who are fighting for these new and vital truths . . . so new that no member of the majority could grasp them.

HOVSTAD: Oh, I see, you've now become a revolutionary.

DR. STOCKMANN: Yes, Mr. Hovstad, that's exactly what I've become. I intend to start a revolution against the lie that the truth belongs only to the majority. What are those truths that the majority claims as their own? They are the truths that are so old they are ready to collapse. But a truth as old as that, gentlemen, is also ready to turn into a lie.

(*laughter and jeers*)

DR. STOCKMANN: Yes, you can believe that I'm right or not. It's up to you. But truth is not the established Methuselah that you think it is. Your everyday truth lives for . . . let me say . . . seventeen or eighteen years, maybe twenty at most . . . rarely longer. And truths as old as that are always thin and frail. However, the majority adopts them only at that stage in their brief life and then recommends them to society as profound spiritual food. But there's no nourishment in food of that kind. I can assure you that is true, because, as a doctor, I know about these things. The truths that the majority adopts are like last year's salt pork . . . like hams that have become rotten, green, and rancid. They are the cause of the moral sickness that has spread throughout our society.

ASLAKSEN: In my opinion, the honorable speaker has departed from his text.

MAYOR: I totally agree with the chairman's observation.

DR. STOCKMANN: Really, Peter, I think you really must be quite mad. I am sticking as close to my text as humanly possible. This is the main point that I am trying to make . . . that it's the masses, this damned majority . . . these are the ones who are poisoning our moral fiber and polluting the ground we walk on.

HOVSTAD: And I suppose that the great liberal majority does this simply because it has enough common sense to believe in those truths which have stood the test of time?

DR. STOCKMANN: My dear Mr. Hovstad, don't talk to me about truths that have stood the test of time. The truths that the masses, the mob, adopt are merely the ones that were formed by the advanced thinkers of our grandparents' days. Those of us who are the advanced thinkers of today don't recognize them anymore. I truly believe that there is only one indisputable truth. It is that no society can be healthy if it feeds on truths that are old and have no meat on their bones.

HOVSTAD: Instead of all these generalizations, why don't you give us some specific examples of these old and meatless truths on which we are subsisting?

(*murmurs of agreement*)

DR. STOCKMANN: Oh, I could give you a whole long list of the damned things, but to start off, I'll just choose one "accepted truth" which is really a damn lie, even though Mr. Hovstad and the *People's Tribune* and all the sycophants at the *Tribune* feed on it all the same.

HOVSTAD: And what is that?

DR. STOCKMANN: It's the doctrine you've inherited from your forefathers, and which you, in your mindless way, continue to promulgate, the doctrine that the common man, the masses, the mob are the living soul of the people . . . that they *are* the people and that the common man—that is, the millions of ignorant and incompetent human beings have the same right to pass judgment, to advise, and to govern as their rare intellectual superiors.

BILLING: Well, by golly that's . . .

HOVSTAD: Make a note of *that*, my fellow citizens.

VARIOUS CITIZENS: Ah, so we're not the people, is that what you're saying? It's only our superiors who have the right to rule? Throw him out! If he doesn't shut up! Out through the door with him!

A CITIZEN: Blow your horn, Evensen.

(*loud blasts from the horn, whistling, and general uproar*)

DR. STOCKMANN: (*when the uproar dies down a little*) Be reasonable, be reasonable. Can't you try to listen to the truth for once in your lives? I'm not asking all of you to agree with me right at this moment! But I thought that Mr. Hovstad would admit that I was right once he'd had a little time to think about it. I mean, Mr. Hovstad claims to be a freethinker.

VOICES: Freethinker? What did he say?

HOVSTAD: (*shouting*) Prove that! Prove that! I have never said that in print!

DR. STOCKMANN: (*pauses*) No, by God, you're right. You've never had the guts to admit it. But, Mr. Hovstad, I won't back you into a corner. So! *I* am openly a freethinker. I am a scientist. So let me tell you all that the *Tribune lies* without shame. It tells you that you, the mob, you, the masses, you, the common people are the heart and soul of this community. It's a lie. A newspaper *lie*. The masses are simply the raw material from which, maybe, someday, individual human beings may be refined.

(*laughter, antagonistic sounds and disturbances*)

DR. STOCKMANN: Well, isn't that what life is like? Just consider the huge difference between a well-bred animal and one that is not. Just look at the common farm chicken. Now, what is such a scrawny piece of garbage worth for its meat? Not very much. And what are its eggs like? Any common or garden crow or jay can lay eggs that are just as good. But if you've got a well-bred Spanish or Japanese hen or a fine pheasant or turkey, you'll see the difference. And let's think about dogs since we human beings have so much in common with them. Think of a dog in the street, one of those flea-bitten, mangy curs that prowl the streets and befoul the walls of our houses. Compare that street dog with, say, a well-bred Labrador whose ancestors have lived in a gentleman's home and that has been fed good food and where it has heard gentle voices and beautiful music. Don't you think the brain of that Labrador is radically different from that of a dog of the streets? Of course it is. It's the offspring of these well-bred animals that people train to perform the most amazing tricks . . . tricks that a common cur could not learn to do even if it stood on its head. (*uproar and laughter*)

A CITIZEN: (*shouts*) So now we're dogs too, are we?

ANOTHER CITIZEN: We're not animals, Doctor.

DR. STOCKMANN: Oh yes, my friend. We *are* animals. But there are very few well-bred animals in our midst, and there is a frightening difference between men who are Labradors and men who are dogs of the street. And that's what I find so amazing. . . . Mr. Hovstad will agree with me as long as we're only talking about four-legged animals.

HOVSTAD: Well, that's what they are, just animals.

DR. STOCKMANN: Fine. But, once I start to apply the rules to two-legged animals, Mr. Hovstad resists the implications. He editorializes in the *Tribune* that the mongrel of the streets is "Best in Show." But that's the way it always goes when a man is obsessed by his blind worship of the masses and cannot see clearly to believe in intellectual superiority.

HOVSTAD: I don't believe in such class distinctions. I come from rural peasant stock, and I am proud that my roots run deep in the masses that you mock.

MANY WORKERS: (*shouting*) Hip hip hooray for Hovstad. Three cheers for Hovstad!

DR. STOCKMANN: The kind of masses I'm talking about are not only to be found at the bottom of the social scale. They teem and swarm all around us, even in the top echelons of society. Just look at your own self-satisfied mayor. My brother, Peter, is as good a representative of the masses as anyone who owns a pair of shoes. (*laughter, hisses, and boos*)

MAYOR: I lodge a protest against these personal attacks.

DR. STOCKMANN: (*ignoring him*) And that isn't because he is the son of a reprobate, an old pirate from Pomerania or thereabouts . . . for that's the truth. . . .

MAYOR: That's ridiculous. It's a lie. I absolutely deny it.

DR. STOCKMANN: Because he thinks the same thoughts his superiors think, and he only echoes their opinions. Men like that are, in essence, just members of the masses. And that's why my magnificent brother, Peter, is, in essence, a common man and, as a consequence, is terrified of liberal thinking.

MAYOR: (*interrupting*) Mr. Chairman!

HOVSTAD: So, it's the intellectual superiors who are the liberals in this country? Is that your new discovery? (*laughter in the audience*)

DR. STOCKMANN: Yes, that is a part of my new discovery. And that is because liberal thinking is almost precisely parallel to morality. And I say that the *Tribune* has no right to promote, day after day, the false doctrine that the masses, the "solid majority," the mob, have a monopoly on liberal thinking and morality . . . and that corruption, vice, and every sort of intellectual depravity are the result of culture oozing out just like that toxic filth that's coming from the tanneries at Moelledal.

(*uproar and lots of interruptions*)

DR. STOCKMANN: (*ignoring them and laughing in his passion*) And yet this same *Tribune* has the gall to preach that the masses and the common mob must be granted an elevated status in society. My God! If what the *Tribune* is preaching were true, then to raise the masses would simply be setting them on the path of moral ruin. But it's lucky for us that the idea that culture saps our moral senses is an old and tired myth. No. It's poverty, it's stupidity, it's being forced to live in filth that do the devil's work. If you have to live in a house where the rooms are airless and the floors not swept—my wife, Katherine, says that the floors should be scrubbed too, but there can be different opinions on that—in a house like that I say that, in two or three years, the inhabitants lose the ability to think moral thoughts and take moral action. The absence of clean air weakens the conscience. As far as I can tell, there's a lack of clean air in many, many houses in this town. If this cursed majority can be so lacking in conscience that it is trying to build the prosperity of this town on a toxic bed of lies and deceit . . .

ASLAKSEN: You can't just hurl an accusation like that against the whole community.

A CITIZEN: I appeal to the chairman to ask the speaker to step down.

VOICES: Yes. Yes. That's right. Make him step down.

DR. STOCKMANN: (*exploding in anger*) Then I'll shout the truth on every street corner. I'll write to the newspapers in other towns. The whole country will be told what is happening here.

HOVSTAD: It sounds as if the doctor wants to destroy this town.

DR. STOCKMANN: Yes. I love this town where I was born so much that I would rather destroy it than see it become prosperous because of a lie!

ASLAKSEN: Those are fighting words!

(*Lots of shouts and whistling. Mrs. Stockmann coughs louder and louder. The doctor does not hear her.*)

HOVSTAD: The man who is capable of wanting to destroy a whole community must be a public enemy.

DR. STOCKMANN: (*increasingly agitated*) If a community lives on lies, it deserves to be destroyed. I say that a town that is home to a community like this ought to be torn down to the ground. All those who live on lies should be exterminated like vermin. This town will end up contaminating the whole country. You will reach a point where the whole country will deserve to be laid waste and, if it gets that bad, then I say to you with all my heart, let the whole country be laid waste, let the whole people be exterminated.

A CITIZEN: You're talking like an enemy of the people.

BILLING: There's the voice of the people, by golly!

CROWD: (*screaming together*) Yes, yes. An enemy of the people! A man who hates his country. He hates the people of this country!

ASLAKSEN: I speak now as a citizen and as a human being. I am deeply shocked by what I have been forced to listen to. Dr. Stockmann has revealed his true self—and in a way I never thought I would hear from him—I'm afraid I must second the views expressed moments ago by respected members of this community. I move that we formalize these views in the following resolution: "This

106

meeting formally declares that the medical officer at the Municipal Baths, Dr. Thomas Stockmann, is an enemy of the people."

(*Huge cheers and applause. The crowd encircles Dr. Stockmann, whistling and jeering. Mrs. Stockmann and Petra stand up. Morten and Eilif fight with some schoolboys who have been jeering too. Some citizens break up the fight.*)

DR. STOCKMANN: (*to those who have been jeering*) You fools! Listen to me. Listen!

ASLAKSEN: (*ringing his bell*) The doctor no longer has the floor. We will have a formal ballot. But to ensure individual privacy, the votes should be written and they should be anonymous. Do you have any clean paper, Mr. Billing?

BILLING: I've got some blue and some white.

ASLAKSEN: (*coming down from the dais*) Good. That'll save time. Tear it up into squares. Yes. Like that. (*to the audience*) Blue means "no," white means "yes." I'll collect the votes myself.

(*The mayor leaves. Aslaksen and some other citizens go around the crowd with paper squares in hats.*)

A CITIZEN: (*to Hovstad*) What's come over the doctor? I mean, what are we to think?

HOVSTAD: Well, you know how hotheaded he is.

ANOTHER CITIZEN: (*to Billing*) You go over to his house a lot. Have you ever noticed . . . does the man drink?

BILLING: I don't know how to answer that, by golly. I mean, there is always some hot toddy on the table for visitors.

ANOTHER CITIZEN: I think he just loses his head now and again.

FIRST CITIZEN: Well, I've heard that madness runs in the family.

BILLING: Could be.

ANOTHER CITIZEN: No. I think it's sheer jealousy. Maybe he wants revenge for something.

BILLING: The other day he did bring up the idea of a raise, but he didn't get it.

CITIZENS: (*together*) Oh, that's what it is!

THE DRUNK: (*in the middle of the crowd*) Gimme a blue one, and I want a white one too.

VARIOUS VOICES: There's that drunk again. Chuck him out!

MORTEN KIIL: Well, Stockmann, you see now what happens if you start monkeying around.

DR. STOCKMANN: I've done my duty.

MORTEN KIIL: What was that you were saying about the tanneries at Moelledal?

DR. STOCKMANN: You heard what I said. That's where all the pollution is coming from.

MORTEN KIIL: From my tannery too?

DR. STOCKMANN: I am sorry to say so, but your tannery is the worst culprit.

MORTEN KIIL: Are you going to print that in the papers?

DR. STOCKMANN: I will hide nothing.

MORTEN KIIL: That's going to cost you, Stockmann. A lot. (*leaves*)

A FAT MAN: (*crossing to Horster, not greeting the women*) Well, Captain. So, you lend out your house to enemies of the people?

HORSTER: I think I can do what I like with my own property.

FAT MAN: Then you'll have no objection if I do the same with mine?

HORSTER: What do you mean?

FAT MAN: You'll hear from me tomorrow. (*leaves*)

PETRA: Captain Horster, isn't that the owner of your ship?

HORSTER: Yes.

ASLAKSEN: (*with the votes in his hands, goes to the dais and rings the bell*) Gentlemen, let me inform you of the results. With only a single dissenting vote . . .

A VOICE: That's the drunk!

ASLAKSEN: With only a single dissenting vote, and that belonging to someone whose sobriety is in question, this assembly of citizens unanimously declares that the medical officer of the baths, Dr. Thomas Stockmann, is an enemy of the people.

CROWD: (*shouts of approval*) Long live our venerable and noble community! (*more cheers*) Long live our worthy and effective mayor who has so loyally ignored the ties of blood. (*cheers*)

ASLAKSEN: The meeting is now adjourned. (*he steps down*)

BILLING: Three cheers for the chairman!

(*the crowd gives three cheers for Aslaksen*)

109

DR. STOCKMANN: My hat and coat, please, Petra. Captain, do you have room on your ship for some passengers to the New World?

HORSTER: For you and your family, Doctor, I'll make room.

DR. STOCKMANN: . . . (*Petra helps him with his coat*) Good. Come along, Katherine. Come on, boys. (*takes Katherine by the arm*)

MRS. STOCKMANN: (*in a whisper*) Thomas, my love, let's go out the back way.

DR. STOCKMANN: Not the back way for me, Katherine. (*raising his voice*) You'll be hearing from your enemy of the people before he brushes off the dust of this town from his feet. I cannot forgive as a . . . certain man once did . . . I can't say, "I forgive you for you know not what you do."

ASLAKSEN: (*shouting*) To compare yourself . . . that's blasphemy, Dr. Stockmann!

BILLING: I'd say so, by Go—I mean, to say such a terrible thing in front of respectable people!

A ROUGH VOICE: And he's threatening us now.

OTHER SPEAKERS: Let's break his windows. Let's chuck him into the sea.

A VOICE: Blow your horn, Evensen.

(*He imitates the sound of the horn a couple of times. Then there are blasts on the real horn. Whistles. Wild shouts. Dr. Stockmann and his family move toward the door. Horster clears their path.*)

CROWD: (*howling after they leave*) Enemy of the people! Enemy of the people! Enemy of the people!

BILLING: (*putting his notes in order*) I'll be damned if I have a drink of toddy with them tonight, by golly.

(*The crowd rushes toward the door. The shouting comes from outside and can be heard from the street.*)

CROWD: Enemy of the people! Enemy of the people! Enemy of the people!

ACT 5

It is morning. Dr. Stockmann's study. Bookshelves and cupboards containing medical supplies line the walls. At the rear is the exit to the hallway. Downstage left is the living room door. The windows on the right wall have been smashed. Dr. Stockmann's desk in the middle of the room is covered with books and papers. The room is a mess.

Dr. Stockmann is in a bathrobe and slippers, and is also wearing his smoking cap. He is crouched down by one of the cupboards raking under it with an umbrella. He finds a stone.

DR. STOCKMANN: (*shouting through to the living room*) Katherine, I found another one!

MRS. STOCKMANN: There'll be lots more.

DR. STOCKMANN: (*putting the stone on a pile of them on the table*) I will treasure these stones. They'll be sacred relics. Eilif and Morten will look at them every day, and when they grow up they'll inherit them. (*continues raking*) Has . . . what the hell's her name? You know, the maid . . . has she been to the window repairman yet?

MRS. STOCKMANN: (*enters*) He told her he wasn't sure he could come today.

112

DR. STOCKMANN: Ha! The truth is, he's afraid.

MRS. STOCKMANN: Yes. Randine thought he was afraid of his neighbors. (*speaking into the living room*) What is it, Randine? Oh, all right. (*goes in and comes back immediately*) There's a letter for you, Thomas.

DR. STOCKMANN: Let me see. (*opens it and reads*) Of course.

MRS. STOCKMANN: Who's it from?

DR. STOCKMANN: The landlord. Notice to quit.

MRS. STOCKMANN: Really? Such a nice man I thought.

DR. STOCKMANN: (*reading*) Says he has no choice. He's very sorry but he daren't do otherwise . . . his fellow citizens. . . . Respect for public opinion . . . obligations to . . . dare not offend certain men of influence. . . .

MRS. STOCKMANN: There, Thomas, you see?

DR. STOCKMANN: Yes, yes, I see. They're all cowards in this town. None of them has the courage to do anything. They're afraid of everyone else. (*tosses the letter on the table*) But it doesn't matter to us, Katherine. We're off to the New World—

MRS. STOCKMANN: Thomas, do you really think that that's a good idea?

DR. STOCKMANN: Am I supposed to stay here when they have branded me as an enemy of the people, pilloried me, broken my windows? And look at this, Katherine—they've torn my trousers too!

MRS. STOCKMANN: Oh no! And they're your best pair too!

DR. STOCKMANN: A man shouldn't wear his best trousers when he goes forth to fight for freedom and truth. Oh, I don't care about the trousers—you can always patch them up for me. It's just that these scum of the earth dare to threaten me as though they were my equals. For the life of me, that's what I can't stomach.

MRS. STOCKMANN: Yes, Thomas, they have treated you shamefully here. But is that a good enough reason to leave the country?

DR. STOCKMANN: Do you think this riffraff isn't as arrogant in other towns around here? Oh, yes, Katherine. One town is as bad as another. To hell with these dogs. Let them snarl. But that's not the worst of it. The worst part is that, in this country, all of it, all the people are slaves to the political system. Of course, it's probably not much better in America. The majority rules there too. And then there's the liberal bias, public opinion, and all the rest of that garbage, but over there the landscape is much larger. They may kill you, but you won't die from slow torture. They don't put a free man in a vise like they do here. And if you want to, you can live in solitude, be a hermit. (*walking around the room*) If only there were some primeval jungle or a little South Sea island that didn't cost very much. . . .

MRS. STOCKMANN: What about the boys, Thomas?

DR. STOCKMANN: (*stopping in his tracks*) You know, Katherine, sometimes you amaze me. Would you prefer for them to grow up in a society like this one? Last night you saw for yourself that half the people are out of their minds, and if the other half haven't lost their minds it's only because they are animals and they have no minds to lose.

MRS. STOCKMANN: But Thomas, my love, you don't think about the consequences of what you say.

DR. STOCKMANN: Ha! Don't I? Don't I tell them the truth? Don't they turn all my ideas upside down? Don't they make right and wrong the same thing so that they can't tell the difference between them? Don't they say that what I know to be true is a lie? But what's really crazy is this: you get grown-up men of the liberal persuasion forming little cabals, and they convince themselves and other people that they are progressive thinkers. I mean, Katherine, isn't that absurd?

MRS. STOCKMANN: Yes. It's all very stupid. But I . . .

(*Petra enters from the living room*)

MRS. STOCKMANN: Back from school already?

PETRA: I've just been fired.

MRS. STOCKMANN: Fired?

DR. STOCKMANN: You too?

PETRA: Mrs. Busk gave me my notice, so I thought I'd better just leave at once.

DR. STOCKMANN: Absolutely right.

MRS. STOCKMANN: I never thought Mrs. Busk was such an unpleasant woman.

PETRA: Oh, she's not unpleasant, Mother. It was quite clear that she didn't enjoy doing it, but she said she dared not do anything else. So, I got fired.

DR. STOCKMANN: (*laughing and rubbing his hands*) Dared not do anything else. Her too. Oh, that's just wonderful.

MRS. STOCKMANN: Well, after all the terrible things that happened last night you can't . . .

PETRA: It wasn't just that. Listen to this.

DR. STOCKMANN: Yes?

PETRA: Mrs. Busk showed me three, yes three letters she got this morning.

DR. STOCKMANN: Anonymous, of course.

PETRA: Yes.

DR. STOCKMANN: They're afraid to even sign their names, Katherine.

PETRA: Two of them said that a gentleman who is often a guest in this house announced in the club last night that I hold excessively free views on various subjects.

DR. STOCKMANN: I hope you didn't deny that.

PETRA: Of course I didn't. In fact, Mrs. Busk has some pretty liberal views herself, especially when we are alone together. But now that this has become public, she just didn't dare to keep me on.

MRS. STOCKMANN: Imagine that! "A gentleman who is often a guest in this house . . ." You see what you get for your hospitality, Thomas.

DR. STOCKMANN: This place is a jungle. We're not going to live here anymore. Pack the bags as quick as you can, Katherine. The sooner we get out of here, the better.

MRS. STOCKMANN: Shhh. I think I hear someone in the hall. Take a look, Petra.

PETRA: (opening the door) Is that you, Captain Horster? Please come in.

HORSTER: (from the hallway) Good morning. I had to come and see how you are doing.

DR. STOCKMANN: (*shaking his hand*) Thank you. That's extremely kind of you.

MRS. STOCKMANN: And thank you for making sure we got back safely last night, Captain Horster.

PETRA: How did you manage to get back to your house?

HORSTER: Oh, I managed. I'm a big man, and their bark is worse than their bite.

DR. STOCKMANN: Yes. They're such . . . cowards. It's amazing. Look here, let me show you something. These are the stones they threw through our windows. Look at them! My God. There are only a couple of good-sized rocks in the whole . . . the rest are just pebbles . . . gravel. And there they were, outside, yelling and screaming, saying they'd beat the life out of me. But did they do anything? No. They don't do anything in this town.

HORSTER: Well, this time that was a good thing, Doctor.

DR. STOCKMANN: Well, yes, but it infuriates me anyway. I mean, if ever there is a need for a serious fight . . . if we have to defend our country, what'll happen is this, Captain Horster: the general public will choose safety first, and this solid majority will run like a flock of sheep. I mean it's really sad . . . it really hurts. . . . No, god damn it! I'm just being stupid. They called me an enemy of the people, so that's what I am going to be, an enemy of the people.

MRS. STOCKMANN: That's something you'll never be, Thomas.

DR. STOCKMANN: Don't be so sure, Katherine. A cruel word is like a dagger in the heart. Those words, I can't get them out of my mind. They're here in the pit of my stomach. They're eating into me like acid, and there is no alkaline to neutralize it.

PETRA: Just laugh at them, Father.

HORSTER: In time, Doctor, people will change their minds about you.

MRS. STOCKMANN: Yes, Thomas. As sure as you are standing there.

DR. STOCKMANN: Maybe. But it'll be too late. Well, that's their problem. They can live like the animals they are. They'll be sorry they drove a man who loves his country into exile. When do you set sail, Captain?

HORSTER: Well, that's what I came to talk to you about. . . . As a matter of fact . . .

DR. STOCKMANN: Has something happened to the ship?

HORSTER: No. It's just that I won't be going with her.

PETRA: They haven't given you the sack?

HORSTER: (*smiling*) Yes, they have.

PETRA: You too?

MRS. STOCKMANN: There, Thomas, you see?

DR. STOCKMANN: Just because I told the truth. Oh, if I'd ever thought that a thing like this could happen!

HORSTER: Don't worry about me. I'll find a job with some other company.

DR. STOCKMANN: But your boss is rich. He's completely independent. Damn it, damn it, damn it!

HORSTER: Usually he's a fair man. He said himself that he'd like to have kept me on. If only he'd dared to. . . .

DR. STOCKMANN: (*laughing*) But he didn't dare. Of course he didn't.

HORSTER: Well, he said it wasn't so easy if you belonged to a party.

DR. STOCKMANN: Well, that's probably the truest word he ever spoke. The party is like a meat grinder. It grinds everyone's brains into a pulp. All you've got in the end is human sausages, all identical.

MRS. STOCKMANN: Now, Thomas, really!

PETRA: (*to Captain Horster*) I just wish you hadn't brought us home. Then this might never have happened.

HORSTER: I have no regrets.

PETRA: (*holding out her hand*) Thank you.

HORSTER: (*to Dr. Stockmann*) What I wanted to tell you was this: if you still want to go, I've thought of another way.

DR. STOCKMANN: That's good. . . . As long as we can get away from here quickly.

MRS. STOCKMANN: Shhh. Wasn't there a knock at the door?

PETRA: I think it's Uncle Peter.

DR. STOCKMANN: Aha! (*shouts*) Come in.

MRS. STOCKMANN: Now, Thomas, my love, promise me . . .

(*the mayor enters*)

MAYOR: (*in the doorway*) Oh, you're busy. I'll come back later.

DR. STOCKMANN: No, no. Please come in.

MAYOR: I wanted to talk with you in private.

MRS. STOCKMANN: We'll go into the living room.

HORSTER: I'll come back later.

DR. STOCKMANN: No, please wait. I want to know more about that. . . .

HORSTER: All right, I'll wait inside.

(*The three of them go into the living room. The mayor says nothing but looks at the broken windows.*)

DR. STOCKMANN: It's a bit drafty in here today, isn't it? You can put your hat on.

MAYOR: Thank you, if you don't mind. (*puts his hat on*) I think I caught a bit of a cold last night. I was shivering.

DR. STOCKMANN: Oh, really? I thought it was pretty warm in there.

MAYOR: I regret that I didn't have the power to prevent those nocturnal excesses.

DR. STOCKMANN: Is that what you came here to tell me?

MAYOR: (*taking out a large envelope*) I have this document for you, from the directors of the baths.

DR. STOCKMANN: Am I to be fired?

MAYOR: From the date of this letter. (*putting it on the table*) This is distressing, but, quite frankly, there was no choice. Given public opinion we didn't dare . . .

DR. STOCKMANN: Didn't dare? I think I've heard that somewhere before.

MAYOR: I beg you to understand your position. From now on you cannot hope to have any medical practice whatsoever in this town.

DR. STOCKMANN: To hell with my medical practice. But what makes you so sure?

MAYOR: The Property Owners Association has drawn up a petition against you, which it is taking from house to house. All respectful citizens are being urged not to use your services, and, I promise you, there will not be one single household that will refuse to sign. They just won't dare.

DR. STOCKMANN: Yes. I have no doubt. But what then?

MAYOR: My advice would be that you leave town for a while.

DR. STOCKMANN: Yes. That's what I'm thinking of doing.

MAYOR: Good. Then when you've had six months or so to think it over, you might, when you've had the time to consider it, you might possibly find it in your heart to issue a short statement . . . admitting your mistakes and expressing your regret. . . .

DR. STOCKMANN: And then, I suppose, I might get my job back?

MAYOR: It's not unthinkable.

DR. STOCKMANN: But what about public opinion, I mean, you daren't go against that?

MAYOR: Well, public opinion is fickle, and, to be frank, it's important to us that you publish this admission in writing.

DR. STOCKMANN: Yes. You'd enjoy that, wouldn't you? But god damn it, don't you remember what I said about such underhanded behavior?

MAYOR: Well, you were in a stronger position then. You believed you had the backing of the whole town.

DR. STOCKMANN: And now the whole town is on my back. But I don't care if the devil himself and his damned wife were sitting on my back. I'll never do it, never.

MAYOR: A family man has no right to do what you are doing. No right, Thomas.

DR. STOCKMANN: No right? There's only one thing that a free man has no right to do. And do you know what that is?

MAYOR: No.

DR. STOCKMANN: No, of course you don't. Then I'll tell you. A free man has no right to wallow in his own filth like an animal, he has no right to turn on himself and spit in his own face.

MAYOR: That sounds reasonable enough, except that there seems to be another explanation for your stubbornness.

DR. STOCKMANN: And what is that?

MAYOR: You know exactly what I mean. But as your brother, as a man of the world, I offer you this advice. Don't hold out too much hope for a future that may not happen.

DR. STOCKMANN: What the hell are you talking about?

MAYOR: Do you really expect me to believe that you don't know the terms of Morten Kiil's will?

DR. STOCKMANN: I know that he is leaving what little money he has to a home for retired workingmen. What's that got to do with me?

MAYOR: Well, first of all, it's not so little. Your father-in-law is a pretty wealthy man.

DR. STOCKMANN: I had no idea.

MAYOR: You didn't? Then I suppose you also have no idea that a large amount of his estate is to be left to your children, and that you and Katherine will be able to live off the interest for the rest of your life? He hadn't told you?

DR. STOCKMANN: No, he hadn't. In fact, all he does is complain about how he has to pay an excessive amount in taxes. Are you sure about this, Peter?

MAYOR: I have an unimpeachable source.

DR. STOCKMANN: But, my God, that means Katherine's future is secure, and the children's. Oh, I must tell her. (*shouts*) Katherine! Katherine!

MAYOR: Shhh. Don't say a word yet.

MRS. STOCKMANN: (*opens the door*) What is it?

DR. STOCKMANN: Nothing, my love. You can go back in.

(*Mrs. Stockmann closes the door*)

DR. STOCKMANN: (*walking around the room*) Their future is secure. I can't believe it. All of them and for the rest of their lives. That's a wonderful feeling. For the rest of their lives. . . .

MAYOR: But that's the catch. Morten Kiil can change that will anytime he chooses.

DR. STOCKMANN: But he won't, my dear Peter. The Badger is much too pleased at the embarrassment I've caused you and your friends.

MAYOR: (*looks at him carefully*) Aha! So that's the reason.

DR. STOCKMANN: What do you mean?

MAYOR: The whole thing is a huge conspiracy. You have accused the authorities in such a vindictive and unprincipled way. You called it truth, but in reality it was your way of getting into that mean-spirited old fool's will.

DR. STOCKMANN: Peter, you are the most disgusting lowlife I have ever met.

MAYOR: Well, it's all over between us now. Your dismissal is final. We have a weapon against you now. (*he leaves*)

DR. STOCKMANN: That filthy . . . god damn it. (*shouting*) Katherine! Scrub the floors. Tell her to bring a bucket. That girl, what the hell's her name? The one with the snotty nose?

MRS. STOCKMANN: (*in the doorway*) Hush, Thomas, please!

PETRA: (*in the doorway*) Father, Grandfather is here. He wants to speak with you in private.

DR. STOCKMANN: Yes, of course. (*goes to door*) Come in, Father.

(*Morten Kiil comes in. Dr. Stockmann closes the door.*)

DR. STOCKMANN: Well, what can I do for you? Sit down.

MORTEN KIIL: No, I won't, thank you. (*looking around*) It looks nice and comfortable in here today, Stockmann.

DR. STOCKMANN: Yes, doesn't it?

MORTEN KIIL: Very nice. Lots of fresh air too. You've got plenty of that oxygen you were talking about last night. Expect your conscience feels pretty good today.

DR. STOCKMANN: Yes, it does.

MORTEN KIIL: I thought so. (*patting his breast pocket*) Do you know what I've got in here?

DR. STOCKMANN: I hope it's a good conscience too.

MORTEN KIIL: No, it's something much better than that. (*takes out a thick folder, opens it, shows him a wad of papers*)

DR. STOCKMANN: (*looking at him in amazement*) Shares in the baths?

MORTEN KIIL: They were easy to come by today.

DR. STOCKMANN: You mean, you've been buying . . . ?

MORTEN KIIL: As many as I could afford.

DR. STOCKMANN: But, my dear sir, the baths are in such a mess, you . . .

MORTEN KIIL: If you do the right thing, you'll soon clean them up.

DR. STOCKMANN: Well, as you can see, I'm doing all that I can, but the people of this town are totally crazy.

MORTEN KIIL: What you said last night was that most of the pollution comes from my tannery. If that is true, then my grandfather and my father before me, and I myself, have been polluting this town for generations past like a trio of angels of death. Do you think I am going to let my reputation be destroyed like that?

DR. STOCKMANN: I'm afraid it looks as if you're going to have to.

MORTEN KIIL: Thank you, but no. I value my name and my reputation. People call me the Badger, or so I'm told. A badger is a filthy animal, isn't it? Well, I'll show them they are wrong. I intend to live clean and die clean.

DR. STOCKMANN: And how are you going to do that?

MORTEN KIIL: Well, you're the one who's going to make me clean, Stockmann.

DR. STOCKMANN: Me?

MORTEN KIIL: Do you know what money I've used to buy these shares? No, how could you? I'll tell you. It's the money Katherine and Petra and the boys are going to get when I'm gone. I've managed to save a little, you understand.

DR. STOCKMANN: (*furious*) You mean, you used Katherine's money for this?

MORTEN KIIL: Yes. It's all been invested in the baths. So, now we'll find out if you are really as stupid as you pretend to be, Stockmann. If you ever say there are toxic creatures coming from my tannery, it'll be just as if you were cutting slices of flesh from your wife's body, and Petra's, and the boys'. But no respectable husband and father would do something like that . . . unless he really was mad.

DR. STOCKMANN: (*walking around the room*) Yes, but I am mad, I am mad.

MORTEN KIIL: But you can't be mad when the welfare of your wife and children is at stake.

DR. STOCKMANN: (*stopping in front of him*) Why didn't you speak to me before you bought all this worthless trash?

MORTEN KIIL: What's done is done.

DR. STOCKMANN: (*wandering around*) If only I weren't so sure. But I know that I'm right. I know.

MORTEN KIIL: (*holding the folder in his hands*) If you persist in this madness, these shares won't be worth much, I can tell you. (*puts the folder back in his pocket*)

DR. STOCKMANN: But damn it, science must be able to find a way, something to stop the pollution, some sort of purifier.

MORTEN KIIL: You mean something to kill these creatures?

DR. STOCKMANN: Yes. Or to make them harmless.

MORTEN KIIL: What about rat poison?

DR. STOCKMANN: No, no. Everyone says this is a figment of my imagination. All right. Let them think like that. Those ignorant, small-minded dogs attacked me, called me an enemy of the people, didn't they? They almost ripped the clothes off my back.

MORTEN KIIL: And smashed your windows.

DR. STOCKMANN: Yes. And then there's this question of my duty to my family. I have to talk to Katherine. She knows about things like this.

MORTEN KIIL: Good idea. She's a sensible woman. Take her advice.

DR. STOCKMANN: (*turning on him*) Why did you have to do such a stupid thing? Gamble with Katherine's money and put me in this dreadful predicament? When I look at you, I think I'm looking at the devil himself.

MORTEN KIIL: Then I'd better be going. But I want an answer by two o'clock. If it's "no," I'm going to hand these shares over to the old people's home, and I'll do it today.

DR. STOCKMANN: And what will Katherine get then?

MORTEN KIIL: Not a red cent.

(*the hallway door is open, and Hovstad and Aslaksen can be seen*)

MORTEN KIIL: Well, now. Look who we have here.

DR. STOCKMANN: (*staring at them*) What the hell? Do you two still have the gall to come and see me?

HOVSTAD: Yes, we do.

ASLAKSEN: We've got something we want to talk to you about.

MORTEN KIIL: (*whispering*) Yes or no . . . and by two o'clock.

ASLAKSEN: (*looking at Hovstad*) Aha!

(*Morten Kiil leaves*)

DR. STOCKMANN: Well, what do you want? Make it snappy.

HOVSTAD: I'm sure you don't feel too kindly toward us. After the stand we took at last night's meeting.

DR. STOCKMANN: You call it a stand? Oh, a wonderful stand. You lay down like a pair of old ladies. Damn the two of you.

HOVSTAD: You can say what you like, but we couldn't do anything else.

DR. STOCKMANN: You didn't dare to do anything else. Isn't that what you mean?

HOVSTAD: As you wish.

ASLAKSEN: But why didn't you give us an inkling? All you had to do was drop a hint to me or Hovstad.

DR. STOCKMANN: Hint? About what?

ASLAKSEN: About why you were doing it.

DR. STOCKMANN: I don't understand.

ASLAKSEN: (*conspiratorially*) Oh yes, you do, Dr. Stockmann.

HOVSTAD: You needn't keep it a secret any longer.

DR. STOCKMANN: (*looking from one to the other*) What in hell's name . . . ?

ASLAKSEN: Pardon me for asking, but isn't your father-in-law going around town buying up all the shares in the baths?

DR. STOCKMANN: He's bought some today, but . . .

ASLAKSEN: You'd have been better off using someone else . . . someone not quite so close to you.

HOVSTAD: And there was no need to do all of this under your own name. There was no need for anybody to know that it was you who was attacking the baths. You should have let me in on it, Dr. Stockmann.

DR. STOCKMANN: (*staring straight in front of him, looking as if he's just been struck by lightning*) Is this possible?

ASLAKSEN: (*smiling*) It seems so, but it needs to be done with a certain amount of subtlety.

HOVSTAD: And it ought to be done by more than one person. A man has less responsibility if he has a partner.

DR. STOCKMANN: (*calmly*) In short, gentlemen, what is it you want?

ASLAKSEN: Mr. Hovstad can explain it better than . . .

HOVSTAD: No, you tell him, Aslaksen.

ASLAKSEN: Well, our idea is this: now that we know the lay of the land, we think we might put the *Tribune* at your disposal.

DR. STOCKMANN: You're not afraid to risk it? What about public opinion? Aren't you afraid we might cause some sort of storm?

HOVSTAD: We will have to ride out that storm.

ASLAKSEN: But you'll have to be quick on the draw, Doctor. As soon as your plan is complete . . .

DR. STOCKMANN: As soon as my father-in-law and I have bought all the shares on the cheap, you mean.

HOVSTAD: Of course. Your principal motive is scientific inquiry, and that's why you're trying to gain control of the baths.

DR. STOCKMANN: Of course. It was scientific inquiry that made me get the old Badger in on this. And then we'll fiddle around with the water system, do a little digging on the beach, and it won't cost the taxpayers a couple of dollars. I think we're going to get away with this, don't you?

HOVSTAD: Yes, I do, especially if you have the *Tribune* backing you up.

ASLAKSEN: In a free society, the press is a force to be feared, Doctor.

DR. STOCKMANN: Exactly. And public opinion too, Mr. Aslaksen. You'll answer for the Property Owners Association?

ASLAKSEN: The Property Owners Association and the Temperance Society, you can be sure of that.

DR. STOCKMANN: But, gentlemen, I am embarrassed to bring this up, but what would you expect me . . .

HOVSTAD: Well, of course we'd like to help you out and charge you nothing, but the *Tribune* is having a rough time of it at the moment. It's an uphill battle, and I'm reluctant to close things down when there are so many important causes that need our support.

DR. STOCKMANN: That would be a hard thing to have to take for a friend of the people like you. (*in a burst of anger*) But I, I am an enemy of the people. (*walking around the room*) Where's that stick? Where the hell did I put my walking stick?

HOVSTAD: What are you talking about?

ASLAKSEN: You're not thinking of . . .

DR. STOCKMANN: (*stopping*) And what if I didn't give you one penny out of my shares? Rich men like me are pretty closefisted with our money, don't forget.

HOVSTAD: And don't you forget that this business with the shares can be taken more than one way.

DR. STOCKMANN: Yes. That would be right up your alley, wouldn't it? If I don't help out the *Tribune*, you'll call my motives into question. You'll hunt me down, you'll bring me down, and choke the life out of me like a dog chokes a rabbit.

131

HOVSTAD: That's the law of nature. Every animal has to fight for its survival. You know that.

ASLAKSEN: It gets its food wherever it can.

DR. STOCKMANN: Then go and see if you can find some in the gutter. (*striding around the room*) Now, heaven be my witness, we'll see which of the three of us is the strongest animal. (*finds his umbrella*) Aha! (*swings it at them*) Now.

HOVSTAD: You wouldn't dare to attack us.

ASLAKSEN: Be careful with that umbrella.

DR. STOCKMANN: Out through the window, Hovstad.

HOVSTAD: (*in the hall doorway*) Have you gone out of your mind?

DR. STOCKMANN: Out through that window, Aslaksen. Jump! Jump! Right now.

ASLAKSEN: (*running around the desk*) Doctor, Doctor, take a hold of yourself. I'm not a well man. I can't take this excitement. (*screaming*) Help! Help!

(*Mrs. Stockmann, Petra, and Captain Horster come in from the living room*)

MRS. STOCKMANN: Thomas, what in heaven's name is going on?

DR. STOCKMANN: (*brandishing the umbrella*) Jump! I tell you, jump! Into the gutter.

HOVSTAD: This is an unprovoked attack. Captain Horster, I call on you to witness. (*runs out through the hallway*)

MRS. STOCKMANN: (*holding on to her husband*) Thomas, for heaven's sake, control yourself.

ASLAKSEN: (*desperately*) Restraint, Doctor, restraint. (*scampers out through the living room*) Oh, dear me!

DR. STOCKMANN: (*throwing away his umbrella*) Damn it, they got away.

MRS. STOCKMANN: But what did they want?

DR. STOCKMANN: I'll tell you later. I've got other things on my mind. (*goes to the table and scribbles on a card*) Take a look at this, Katherine, what do you see?

MRS. STOCKMANN: (*reading*) No, no, no. What does that mean?

DR. STOCKMANN: I'll tell you later. (*handing Petra the card*) Here, Petra, tell that snotty-nosed girl to run up to the Badger's house and give him this as quickly as she can. Hurry!

(*Petra leaves*)

DR. STOCKMANN: Well I've had visits from all the devil's messengers today, every single one of them. But now I'm going to sharpen my pen and turn its dagger's point against them. I'll dip it in venom and in gall. And I'll hurl my inkstand at their ignorant skulls.

MRS. STOCKMANN: But, Thomas, we're about to leave.

(*Petra returns*)

DR. STOCKMANN: Well?

PETRA: She's gone with it.

DR. STOCKMANN: Good. About to leave, did you say? No, by God, we're not leaving. We're staying right here, Katherine.

PETRA: Staying here?

MRS. STOCKMANN: In this town?

DR. STOCKMANN: Yes. This is my battlefield, it's right here that the battle must be fought, and it's right here that I will be the victor. As soon as you've patched my trousers, I'm going to go into town and look for a house. We must have a roof over our heads in the winter.

HORSTER: I can let you have my house.

DR. STOCKMANN: Would you?

HORSTER: Of course. There are lots of rooms, and I'm hardly ever there.

MRS. STOCKMANN: Oh, Captain Horster, how kind of you.

PETRA: Thank you so much.

DR. STOCKMANN: (*pressing his hand*) Thank you, thank you. Well, that's one problem solved. I'm going to start my campaign right away. Oh, Katherine, there's so much to be done. But, it's lucky that I'll be able to spend all my time on it. Take a look at this. I've been sacked from the baths.

MRS. STOCKMANN: Ah well, that was to be expected.

DR. STOCKMANN: And they are trying to take away my medical practice too. All right. Let them try. At least I can keep my poor patients. And if they're the ones who can't pay, well, God knows, they're the ones who need me the most. But, by God, they're going to have to listen to me. I'll be preaching to them in season and out of season . . . as it says somewhere or other.

MRS. STOCKMANN: Oh, Thomas, Thomas, surely you can now see what a lot of good preaching does.

DR. STOCKMANN: Sometimes you amaze me, Katherine. Do you think I would let myself be chased from the battlefield by public opinion, the solid majority, and such hogwash? No, sir. What I want to do is really simple. It's straightforward. It's easy. All I want to do is knock it into the heads of these dogs that liberals are the most treacherous enemies of freedom, that party agendas strangle every new and living truth, that expediency and self-interest turn morality and justice on their heads. In the end, life here becomes unbearable. Well, Captain Horster, do you think I might be able to get people to understand that?

HORSTER: I think you might. I don't really understand these things myself.

DR. STOCKMANN: Well, the real point is this: it's the party bosses that we've got to get rid of. A party boss is like a . . . ravenous wolf. . . . He needs a certain number of young lambs to devour each year if he is to survive. Look at Hovstad and Aslaksen. How many innocent and vital young idealists do you think they've devoured, or else they have mauled and savaged them till all they're good for is to be property owners or subscribers to the *Tribune.* (*sits on the table*) Come over here, Katherine. Look how beautiful it is. The sun is shining through our windows today, and you can smell this wonderful, fresh spring air wafting in on us.

MRS. STOCKMANN: My dear Thomas, if only we could live on sunshine and springtime air.

DR. STOCKMANN: Well, you may have to pinch pennies and scrape a little bit, but we'll get through it. That's the least of my worries. No, what I'm afraid of is that I don't know of anyone else who loves freedom . . . who is sufficiently unplebeian to carry on after me.

PETRA: Don't worry about that, Father. You'll find someone sometime. Look, here are the boys. (*Eilif and Morten enter*)

MRS. STOCKMANN: They've given you the day off from school?

MORTEN: No. During recess we had a fight with some other boys and so . . .

EILIF: That's not true. The other boys fought with us.

MORTEN: Yes. So I said to Dr. Roerlund that I thought it would be better if we didn't come to school for a few days.

DR. STOCKMANN: (*snapping his fingers and jumping from the table*) That's it! By heaven, that's it! Neither of you will ever set foot in that school again.

EILIF AND MORTEN: We're not going to school?

MRS. STOCKMANN: But, Thomas . . .

DR. STOCKMANN: Never, I tell you. I'll teach you myself. You won't learn a damn thing . . .

MORTEN: Hurrah.

DR. STOCKMANN: But I can make you free men, aristocrats. Petra, you have to help me.

PETRA: Yes, Father, of course.

DR. STOCKMANN: And we'll hold school in the same room where they branded me an enemy of the people, but we'll need more pupils. I need at least a dozen to start off with.

MRS. STOCKMANN: You won't find them in this town.

DR. STOCKMANN: We'll see about that. (*to the boys*) Do you know any children of the streets, you know, urchins?

EILIF: Oh yes, Father, I know lots of them.

DR. STOCKMANN: That's great. Get hold of a few of them for me. I'm going to experiment with street puppies. Some of them have good heads on their shoulders.

EILIF: But, what will we do when we've become free men . . . aristocrats?

DR. STOCKMANN: Then, my boys, you'll drive all those damned politicians into the Atlantic Ocean. (*Eilif looks somewhat doubtful, but Morten jumps up and down and cheers*)

MRS. STOCKMANN: All I hope is that the politicians won't drive you out, Thomas.

DR. STOCKMANN: Are you mad, Katherine? Drive me out? Now that I am the strongest man in the town?

MRS. STOCKMANN: The strongest man . . . now?

DR. STOCKMANN: Yes. I'll go one step further. I'm now one of the strongest men in the world.

MORTEN: Hurrah.

DR. STOCKMANN: (*lowering his voice*) Shh. You can't talk about it yet, but I've made a great discovery.

MRS. STOCKMANN: Not again.

DR. STOCKMANN: Yes. (*gathering them around him and whispering*) The fact is, you see, that the strongest man in the world is the man who stands most alone.

MRS. STOCKMANN: (*smiling and shaking her head*) Oh, Thomas.

PETRA: (*warmly, clasping his hands*) Father.

BOOKS IN THE PLAYS FOR PERFORMANCE SERIES
(alphabetical by author)

Aristophanes, *Lysistrata*
Pierre Augustin de Beaumarchais, *The Barber of Seville*
Pierre Augustin de Beaumarchais, *The Marriage of Figaro*
George Büchner, *Woyzeck*
Anton Chekhov, *The Cherry Orchard*
Anton Chekhov, *Ivanov*
Anton Chekhov, *The Seagull*
Anton Chekhov, *Three Sisters*
Anton Chekhov, *Uncle Vanya*
Thomas Dekker, *The Shoemaker's Holiday*
Euripides, *The Bacchae*
Euripides, *Iphigenia in Aulis*
Euripides, *Iphigenia Among the Taurians*
Euripides, *Medea*
Euripides, *The Trojan Women*
Georges Feydeau, *Paradise Hotel*
Carlo Goldoni, *The Servant of Two Masters*
Henrik Ibsen, *A Doll's House*
Henrik Ibsen, *An Enemy of the People*
Henrik Ibsen, *Ghosts*
Henrik Ibsen, *Hedda Gabler*
Henrik Ibsen, *The Master Builder*
Henrik Ibsen, *When We Dead Awaken*
Henrik Ibsen, *The Wild Duck*
Marivaux, *The Dispute*
Christopher Marlowe, *Doctor Faustus*
Molière, *The Bourgeois Gentleman*
The Mysteries: Creation
The Mysteries: The Passion
Luigi Pirandello, *Enrico IV*
Luigi Pirandello, *Six Characters in Search of an Author*
Budd Schulberg, *On the Waterfront*
Mary Shelley, *Frankenstein*
Sophocles, *Antigone*
Sophocles, *Electra*
Sophocles, *Oedipus the King*
Sophocles, *Oedipus at Colonus*
August Strindberg, *The Father*
August Strindberg, *Miss Julie*
Heinrich von Kleist, *The Prince of Homburg*